SIDE STREET: SAN FRANCISCO

Touted as the promised land, San Francisco is a city known for, among other things, its fancy addresses—an architectural and social wonderland.

Stories of crookedness, sex, violence, fraud, murder, illicit love, and kinky triangles among the rich fill the annals of the city's records. Also, the newspapers.

All of these stories have been told with tinsel and flashing covers, and with lawsuits for libel. But, San Francisco has another facet not mentioned in the society columns and about which few books are written.

The side streets.

Side Street: San Francisco

PROCTOR JONES

SIDE STREET:

SAN FRANCISCO

Published by Proctor Jones Publishing Company, San Francisco, CA.

Cover design by Joseph Cleary, Orinda, CA.

Library of Congress Catalog Card No. 89–091212
ISBN 0–9608860–6–0

DEDICATION

Dedicated to love . . . wherever found.

INTRODUCTION

For whatever purpose, there are those in far-off places who work their lives away just to get to San Francisco.

Some drift there with no plan. Many come as tourists. Some are sent out from the East as district managers of large companies. Some drag their family fortunes with them. Some arrive because economic adversity in Oshgosh or Elyria or Johnson City has forced the search for a place not requiring heavy underwear.

Some just dream about the crenellated city by the Bay.

Touted as the promised land, San Francisco is a city known for, among other things, its fancy addresses. Nob Hill, Russian Hill, Pacific Heights, Broadway, and Sea Cliff all make it an architectural and social wonderland.

Stories of crookedness, sex, violence, fraud, murder, illicit love, and kinky triangles among the rich fill the annals of the city's records. Also, the newspapers.

Of course, there are the seldom-mentioned philanthropists, businessmen, important members of private clubs, the Junior Leaguers, and the fourth estate. Paragons!

All of their stories have been told with tinsel and flashing covers, and with lawsuits for libel. But, San Francisco has another facet not mentioned in the society columns and about which few books are written.

The side streets.

Except for the sordid and some bowling scores, life on the side streets of the city—though interwoven in a thousand ways with the town, its seldom-seen rich, its transportation system, its sewers, its parks—is lost to the newspaper record.

People on the side streets die without mention in the obituaries and such oversight matters very little to the we-take-care-of-our-own-kids set, who scarcely have time to clean t-shirts, change diapers, wash underwear, provide bandaid services, scramble to the grocery store, put out breakfast and dinner, wrap a working man's lunch, or clean out a clogged drain.

People on the side streets may have time for the funnies, but sometimes even the cost of the newspaper denies that. Besides, soap operas can be listened to for free—above the noise of a cheap washing machine.

People like this cannot know that all the strife, struggle, and surrender that takes place on their side street, also takes place in the palaces as well. The difference, of course, is that the frustration on the side street is life itself and not just fleeting inconvenience.

The side street population must work very hard for a living leaving time for very little else.

But, there is time! Time even to live double lives.

Add that to the luster that is San Francisco!

For the troubled, in faraway places, a relative living in San Francisco is often a beacon-light in the storm. And that is what Leona Remmer was to her sister Marian in Tulsa, Oklahoma.

CHAPTER ONE

Leona and Marian were born in San Francisco toward the end of World War II. During the war, their father, Chip Larsen, worked as a machinist at one of the San Francisco Bay shipyards. Their mother, Alice, had been employed as a riveter at the same place. The two had married.

After the war, Chip followed his wartime foreman to work at San Francisco's Hunter's Point shipyard for the Navy.

Alice busied herself having two daughters. It was presumed that each had the same father, but, as the character of the girls developed, that premise became open to question. Although Leona and Marian loved each other as sisters, they were really quite different.

Marian, the younger, was dark haired and, like her mother, a free, gregarious spirit. Leona, the older sister, was blonde, like her father, steady, and, compared with Marian, quiet.

They grew up in the Noe Valley neighborhood of San Francisco close to the school the girls eventually attended and convenient to Hunter's Point as well.

Chip came from Bucyrus, Ohio, a standing family joke. Alice was from Nevada. Wartime opportunities on the West Coast had beckoned both. They liked the climate. With the end of the war, they just stayed on. When Chip retired and both girls had married, for better or for worse, he and Alice moved back to Bucyrus. A mistake. They were killed on an icy highway during their first winter.

During the troubles in Viet Nam, and while the family was still in residence in Noe Valley, Marian had aggressively latched on to Harold Fouts, a sailor who migrated to the Navy from the family farm in Oklahoma. Marian was very young. He was some twelve years her senior. No persuasion could be brought to bear to discourage her from marrying him.

Although he was far from being an albino, he did suffer from a similar eye problem. He could not stand bright lights or sunshine. Somehow this eye problem had slipped by the recruiting officer and the medics. When it was discovered, Harold was given an early convenience discharge, notwithstanding the urgent demands of the Vietnamese conflict. He took Marian back to Oklahoma where he landed a job working for the United Parcel Service.

He was quiet and his glasses gave him a serious look. At first, Marian could not get enough of Harold. However, what flame they had in their first sexual contacts flickered as the early months of marriage passed. Still, by the end of the second year, he was a worn person and she was the mother of Mavis, named after one of Marian's childhood friends.

As time went on, Marian had managed to make up for her husband's shortcomings by leading a life full of fantasy salted with some actuality.

Leona, on the other hand, had almost accepted her lot. She was a good homebody and her two little boys meant the world to her. She was willing to give her husband credit for their generation, but that was all.

Leona and Ralph Remmer were brought together under the most promising of circumstances.

Ralph, a happy, unmarried man, and a stranger in town, had made the mistake of going to a dance sponsored by the Little Sisters of the Good Shepherd. Leona had met him there. He looked quite tall to Leona and had a pleasant smile born in vacancy. Later, he came by the house. As Marian was away at the time, Leona had the field to herself. Ralph fell.

He, like Harold, had started off all right, but, in the press of living-making over the years, he had fallen into a rut. He was a butcher. He accepted his meat cleaver and the South San Francisco Holiday Sureway Supermarket as his life.

Ralph chose to be molded by his chopping block instead of his wife. As time went on, he developed a coarseness, the seeds of which,

Leona, in her first dreams of love, had not recognized. Whatever fatherly things he did for their children were generally directed by Leona.

The first blush gone between Ralph and Leona left not very much to follow. Or, so it appeared.

Leona, during these early years of marriage, remained trim and neat. Her blonde hair was loose and curly and she had a full little figure. Her legs alone could have won her a first prize. Eventually, all of this was completely lost on Ralph.

CHAPTER TWO

Leona Remmer's problem was to find a house in San Francisco for her sister Marian. Marian's husband, Harold, was having some difficulty with his U.P.S. job and had been given a choice of either working for one of the moving companies in Tulsa or going out to a night-shift job at U.P.S. in San Francisco. Although the moving company job would keep Harold and his family in Tulsa, it didn't take him long to realize that it would entail hard work. He chose the night-shift assignment. This, of course, meant that he and the family would have to relocate in San Francisco. Marian had written this in a long letter to her sister.

Leona immediately busied herself with her sister's cry for help. Looking through the for-rent ads, she had gone to look at several dingy places, the prices of which were within her sister's budget. At last, one ad paid off.

Blonde Leona said, "Yes, we'll take it. My younger sister and her little daughter will love it." She smiled her pretty smile. "She and her family are moving here from Tulsa." Leona was all business.

The real estate agent was relieved and pleased to have this marginal property rented so quickly.

Leona thought that the house looked as though whoever was about to leave it had given its future slight concern. The place had a musty odor, mixed with some sort of cheap aftershave lotion.

It seemed strange to her that the living room was being used as a bedroom. There was no rug and the bed was a cross between a sleeping bag and a rubber air mattress. An alarm clock radio was on a box by the bed. The box itself was covered with a navy-blue motel towel.

A fancy color t.v. set, along with a wooden rocker, also graced the otherwise sparsely furnished scene.

Leona noticed that the kitchen did not give signs of any culinary activity. On the side of the drainboard were a few toilet articles, an odd-looking hairbrush, and an electric curling iron. She gave the place a quick eye and figured that the dirt and disorder could be easily handled. In this department, she was an expert.

CHAPTER THREE

In humid Tulsa, Harold Fouts, the husband of Leona's sister, peered out through his heavy bottle-bottomed glasses upon the U.P.S. shipping dock which had been his bread and butter for the last few years, since he left the Navy. That he had never become part of the Tulsa U.P.S. family didn't bother him in view of his transfer to San Francisco.

He liked shoving around the U.P.S. delivery parcels. He was upset about the night-shift business, but he figured that once he had some experience there, he would be able to get himself reassigned.

As he was daydreaming about his future, one of his fellow workers came up to him and asked if he would like to join the poker game that evening. Embarrassed, because he didn't have the ten dollars on him to get into the game, he mumbled something about he'd see.

He called Marian who, at that very moment, was resting at her kitchen table in her sweltering kitchen in one of Tulsa's parboiled, less attractive suburbs. Her raven hair was elastic-banded into a jaunty ponytail and she was sitting on a kitchen stool smoking a cigarette and sipping a beer. She was also perspiring. Bare to the waist, and not much covering the rest of her, she was in the process of packing her limited supply of china for the anticipated move.

Although the heat had wilted her, Marian was a vibrant woman. There was a feline fierceness about her: a fierceness of rebellion against her kitchen, her husband Harold, the heat, and the steamy street on which they both lived.

The phone rang. She answered, slouched over the kitchen counter.

"Yeah?" she invited. Then she recognized Harold's voice. "Oh, you. What'd'ya want?"

"I need ten bucks for the game tonight. You got the car . . . I'll meet you at the shipping entrance."

"Up yours, Harold." She banged the receiver down, frustrated.

Marian's topless bikini was evidence of her wishful thinking.

While her six-year old daughter Mavis attended an afternoon playschool, the mother was hoping to be interrupted by the postman or a meter reader. She didn't much care which one. She also had friends who regularly checked the interests of the various public utility companies.

She surveyed her kitchen through narrowed eyes. Grocery boxes and old newspapers had been pressed into service to transport her ill-appointed belongings to San Francisco. She planned to head west with Mavis and stay with her sister Leona until a place could be found for them to live. Harold would stay on at the Tulsa U.P.S. loading dock until the month was out.

CHAPTER FOUR

In sunny California, Leona's husband, balding Ralph Remmer, a bulky, round-faced man of 40, had a job as a butcher at the Holiday Sureway's meat counter in South San Francisco. He cleaned his fat hands against the soiled surface of his butcher's apron.

"Yeah, yeah, Mrs. Wilbur. A nice one. Yeah, a nice one. Just like you like, Mrs. Wilbur." With his heavy, tattooed forearm, he then wielded a meat cleaver. He made some deep cuts into a piece of meat under his paw, leaving large amounts of fat in place. He slapped what he had cut onto a pink piece of paper and placed it on an automated scale nearby. He checked the price and wrote it in large, childish numbers on the paper which was to transport the meat to the Holiday Sureway cash register and then to Mrs. Wilbur's kitchen, and so on through his work day.

During the afternoon, in her row house in the Richmond district, Leona sat down at her kitchen table and wrote Marian about the place she had found.

"*It's not the cat's meow,*" she penned, "*but it's near to us and it's near Golden Gate Park.*"

She addressed the letter, looked around for a stamp, found one, licked it, and put it in place. Seeing that the children were playing in the backyard, she figured she could make the post box at the corner and get back before any crisis could arise.

At four-thirty, she put together a macaroni and ground-chuck casserole. She opened a can of peaches, put them in a bowl, and placed them in the refrigerator. The kids could have cookies for dessert.

About six-fifteen, heavy Ralph came home, his 1957 Chevrolet just making it into the garage where it kept company with clotheslines, furnace pipes, wash tubs, and the hot water heater. Indistinguishable litter and treasures had been forced to the sides so that the car would fit and still leave room for Ralph. He closed the garage door and crunched up the rickety basement stairs, emerging behind the stove in the kitchen.

Leona had already started the dinner and was putting the eating utensils and paper napkins on the table.

"Hi, honey," she greeted, without turning around.

He grunted a wheezed greeting and went to the refrigerator. Finding a beer, he opened it and took one long gulp. He then stripped to his undershirt.

"Brought you some hot dogs," he belched.

"Goodie," replied Leona with forced enthusiasm.

Five-year old Bubba and three-year old Harvey had the t.v. going so loudly that every word could be heard clearly by the neighbors. Ralph stepped out of the kitchen into the nondescript living room.

"O.K., kids, can it," he belched again.

Leona, pushing back her hair, announced dinner. The troop, including Ralph, went directly to the kitchen table.

Leona knew that there was a night football game at seven. She didn't know who was playing and she didn't care. But, she knew that Ralph did.

Dinner was eaten down to the last peach so fast and with so little comment that Leona wondered why she had not just served up cold beans.

"I found a house for Marian and Harold," she volunteered.

"Yeah? Good. When do they get here?" Ralph asked.

"I guess Marian will come in a week or so. She and Mavis will stay with us for a few days. Then Harold will be here around the fifth with the furniture."

"Lucky you found a place. Where is it?"

"About four blocks from here, toward the Park."

"That's a hell of a thing."

"What's that?"

"I said 'hell.' Why didn't you just find them something in Redwood City?"

"Oh, come on Ralph. You and Harold get along great."

"Yeah."

And so it went, with the children looking first at the father-figure and then at the mother. Some jam and bread had been added to the children's feast, which was now clearly part of Bubba's chin and sweater.

Ralph ate all that was prepared for him without comment. He reminded Leona of the hot dogs as if he had secured the pearl of great price for her.

He ate some more food, rose from the table abruptly, and, taking another beer from the refrigerator, went to his chair in front of the t.v. He promptly switched on the football game.

Leona fussed with the kids and finally herded them upstairs to bed. On their way, each went to their father for a good night kiss which was administered without loss of one blink of television. Finally, the upstairs was quiet. By the time the game was in its final throes, Ralph was in a glossy state but more pleasant than he had been on his arrival home.

"So, skinny Harold's coming," he grunted.

"Yes, and your friend Marian," rejoined Leona.

"For Chrissake, Leona, don't you ever forget anything?"

"Listen, Ralph. There are some things you make unforgettable."

"The hell you say."

"The hell I say, and if you start it again, I'll leave and take the kids to your mother in Sacramento."

"Promises, promises."

And he banged off the t.v. set. "I'm going to bed."

He headed up the stairs.

Leona turned out the lights, checked the stove, and locked the kitchen door. Then she went upstairs. Ralph was already in the bathroom.

She sat down on the side of the bed and kicked off her shoes. Her dress slipped from her tired but nonetheless attractive body. She reached around and undid her bra. She went to the closet and hung up these items without ceremony. She pulled her faded nightgown from its hook and slipped it over her head.

Ralph returned from the bathroom dressed in what Nature gave him, which wasn't much.

"It's all yours," he invited.

She looked at him and figured he meant the bathroom.

"Thanks."

She ran the bath and luxuriated in it for a long few minutes, toweled herself off, creamed her face, slipped into her nightgown for the second time, and gave her face an admiring look in the mirror as she removed the cream with cotton. She turned off the bathroom light.

As Ralph had already turned off the bedroom light, she found her way in the darkness to her side of the bed.

"Night-night, Ralph," she said, out of habit.

"Yeah," said Ralph.

The two met in the middle of the bed, and, without preliminaries, he mounted her in the time-honored fashion. Leona pretended surprise and withstood the short moment of his onslaught. He snorted and rolled over. She thought of the sausages downstairs. He changed his position, pulling on the covers, which, she had learned from experience, to hold onto for dear life.

Ralph was out of it. He snorted again and then began to purr. It was his way of snoring. Leona looked up at the street-light pattern on the ceiling and thanked God for her children.

Pushing the pillow under her arm, she fell asleep with the innocence of a person completely unaware of the urban turmoil and crookedness beyond the life of her safe little side street.

CHAPTER FIVE

Business in San Francisco is run at several levels. Most of the heavy business is done at the behest of out-of-towners. Interests in New York, Chicago, Dallas, Houston, Los Angeles, and, more and more, Hong Kong and Tokyo.

There are a wide variety of smaller businesses in San Francisco. Most are honest and ordinary, but some are profitable con games and downright dishonest. The Mayor of this glistening town, Adrian Belpierre, for all of his ancient and diminutive elegance, had his hand in the latter. A rather big hand for such a little man.

His harvest, garnered from the generous who wished to remain in "business," was deposited in a substantial foundation which the Mayor had established for the benefit of San Francisco widows and orphans.

The Mayor was in charge of this fund and his was a most generous hand. Widows whose names had never graced a marriage register were the object of recorded kindnesses beyond measure. Children, also beneficiaries, were listed as living in far-off places.

The marriage register may have been missed, but the obituaries were not. The passings of husbands were noted and filed with the widow's application for help. Some of these obituaried husbands were marked down as accomplishing unheard of wonders. Unheard of, indeed! They had never happened at all.

Details of the fund were managed under the guiding hand of the Mayor's executive assistant, Clarissa Winship, a spinster—a good choice, and one without a conflict of interest as she was neither an orphan nor likely to become a widow.

She was a tall, mannish blonde. Her voice, cultivated by tobacco in the form of cigarettes, gave her masculine authority. She ran her show from the Mayor's Office providing the crucial votes which cemented the Mayor's powerful position.

Obviously, a distribution system of any substance would involve more than the business capacities of one person, no matter how capable. Assistance came to Ms Winship in a most unlikely fashion

The collection of the town's garbage and dry waste matter was undertaken at one time by many companies, some of whom specialized. One enterprising Irishman owned a pig farm on the windswept hills south of San Francisco. To feed his pigs, he made the rounds of the hotels. Actually, he did business at both the front door and the back door, selling his hams and pig's feet at the front door and collecting whatever remained at the back door, completing a perfect cycle. As this fellow grew older, he began to realize that there was business to be done in other parts of town and he received from the County Supervisors the right to collect garbage from homes in one of the city's districts.

It didn't take him long to realize that some garbage bills were never paid. He was advised to lien property which was in arrears. Many times, these properties came up for tax sale. As an interested party, he was always informed.

He became friendly with the politicians, making appropriate contributions to their various campaigns. Eventually he had the contract for three of the five city garbage districts.

As his business increased, he hired more and more men and he bought more and more vehicles. He also had to establish an office force to deal with all the paper work his extended business interests engendered.

For some time, he had his eye on one of his employees as a possible supervisor George Rizzo had come to America as a small child with his parents. They were Sicilians.

On the pig farm where he eventually found employment, he worked through various jobs until finally he was driving a garbage truck. Nobody knew more about the garbage business than little George Rizzo. He was everywhere!

As the frailities of old age crept up on the Irishman, he gave more and more responsibility to George Rizzo. Finally, Rizzo was General Manager of the garbage company. The old man, by this time, was immersed in a real estate business spawned from his tax sale purchases over the years. Although he felt that he had come up in society, he kept a weather eye on his garbage business, keeping his office space and his title as President. This never bothered Rizzo as he operated without interference.

A contract for the whole town had never been politicked. George Rizzo did that, too. He approached City Hall and soon was in conference with Clarissa Winship. Clarissa, it seemed, was in control of the Supervisorial votes necessary to confirm the garbage contract for the whole town.

Clarissa initiated him into the eleemosynary efforts of the Mayor's Widows and Orphans Fund. At first, Rizzo tried to get away by making a token contribution, but, as his matter dragged on with no resolution, he finally realized that more was expected of him And when he made his appropriate payment, the doors opened and his company received the City contract.

But, that is not all that happened.

In his Italianate way, he had dislodged something in Ms. Clarissa Winship. As he was a small man, it may have been part of her latent mother-instinct.

They became friends, indeed political allies. He soon became part of the petty graft department controlled by Clarissa. One small taste of that and he realized that more important things could be accomplished. Clarissa herself was not idle.

She began to wonder how George Rizzo could be involved in some of the business workings of the Widows and Orphans Fund. When she thought she had Rizzo's confidence, she asked him point blank if he would like to get in on some of the action in which the Mayor took such a great interest. George did not have to think twice. He became a partner.

Friends in Florida, whom the Mayor never saw, were also large contributors to the Widows and Orphans Fund. What they had to sell posed the problem which worried Clarissa Winship. They operated a distribution chain for the sale of snow in sunny California. The chain extended right to and through the Mayoral palace of Adrian Belpierre. The increased volume which was promised would put a strain on the system with which Clarissa had been working. Rizzo was the answer. That is, Rizzo and his trucks. By now, she knew that she could trust Rizzo because he was in so deeply with his payoffs for his garbage contract.

George Rizzo thought that he alone was going to participate in whatever action presented itself and when Clarissa outlined to him her idea for the garbage trucks, he didn't quite get it for a moment, but, when he did, he signed on.

Rizzo's garbage trucks doubled in brass: on the one hand, the courteous minions of public hygiene and, on the other, the dope peddler's winged Mercury.

Who, in listening to the grinding up of the City's waste would see in these mammoth machines the handmaiden of civic depravity? Well, that's what they were. The flotilla covered the whole Bay Area. A truck would be ordered to stop somewhere along its route. Friendly hands, appearing to off-load garbage, would make the delivery of goods already paid for through Mr. Rizzo's office.

Not since the last spike was laid in Utah, completing the trans-America railroad, was there such a demand for the poppy's product.

And, George Rizzo was the local station master.

Dope, garbage, and City Hall. A great combination!

CHAPTER SIX

In San Francisco's neatly platted Richmond district, covered in the haze of morning fog, in the middle of an alley, was a large garbage truck. Its attendant, a tall and bronzed young garbageman, bent down to look into an old mailbox from which he extracted a bulky envelope. He scarcely looked at it. However, as a car backfired and a dog barked, he did give a quick look up and down the alley hoping that he had not been seen.

He went to the cab of his M-1 garbage truck, opened the door, and pulled out a parcel wrapped in brown paper. So insignificant was the wrapping that no one would have thought to have picked it up had it fallen on the sidewalk or into the gutter. Again, looking over his shoulder, he placed it in the old mailbox, and closed the lid securely.

He returned to his truck and, with a great deal of noise, drove away. With his non-English-speaking assistant, Tony De Bono had finished his day which had started with the sunrise at 4:30 a.m. Tony's route took him five hours.

He was a large man, with broad shoulders,

thin hips, soft eyes, and a big smile. He had heavy, square hands. His nut-brown hair was neatly in place as if it had just been marcelled. He looked like a healthy, Italian opera tenor which pleased his Genovese mother.

His I.Q. was something under l00, enough to work with, but not quite enough to secure advancement. He did his job, had his favorite cat houses, and, occasionally, on Sunday, he went to an early movie. Normally, he sat through a film twice, getting his money's worth and, sometimes, by lingering near the popcorn machine, he picked up a girl.

He walked with an exaggerated air of confidence, not a swagger, just an I-know-where-I'm-going walk.

His uncle, who had a broad career in garbage collection, had arranged for Tony's employment. Once Tony was broken into the job, the uncle gave him a short course on the fringe benefits of the trade. This involved women. Married women, some of whom felt trapped by inattentive husbands, and some of whom had attentive husbands but realized the dividends which can come from extended connections such as Tony offered.

Tony with the big smile seemed to satisfy everybody, including his employer.

He headed his garbage rig for the incinerator plant. He swung it into the company garage and handed it over to the man responsible for emptying it.

"How did it go, Tony?" his friend asked, climbing into the driver's seat.

"Lots of it," responded big Tony, walking away.

The cab door slammed shut and the truck headed for the big incinerator. Tony could have done it just as easily, but the local unions had a special category of garbage worker known as an internal handler. Tony's non-English-speaking assistant now became the special handler's assistant.

When Tony left his truck, he walked to the office of the General Manager, George Rizzo. As he entered the outer office, he noticed that Thelma, the General Manager's dishwater-blonde secretary, was bending over a low file drawer. He slipped up in back of her and gave her a suggestive pat on the backside. Her reaction was immediate.

In the course of resuming her upright position, she tightened her small chin and armed herself to do battle. She turned with fire in her grey eyes, which, when she recognized her assailant, turned to limpid pools.

"Oh, you," she laughed, and he gave her a little squeeze while asking if the boss was in.

"Yes, damn it," she hissed.

Thelma Welch wanted to quit her job, as she had experienced George Rizzo's depravity. She couldn't quit because, in a fading market for her particular talents, she had no place to go.

She was right in the center of an operation of which she had very little understanding, except that she knew that if George Rizzo was mixed up in it, it had to be bad.

Tony walked into the boss's office. George Rizzo was on the phone with his back to the door. On hearing Tony come in, he swung his muscular little body around.

"O.K., O.K.," he said hoarsely into the phone. "O.K., don't worry. We'll take care of it. Sorry we missed you. O.K., yeah, yeah. Goodbye."

Looking up at Tony with his small, ferret-like eyes he said, "Forty-two missed a can in the Sunset and you'd think that City Hall burned down."

He nervously arranged something on his desk, then rose and closed the office door.

George Rizzo was built like a tension spring. His hair was thinning. You noticed his ears and nose.

"Well?" he asked. "You make the delivery?"

"Sure," said Tony. "And a pick-up. Here's your envelope."

George Rizzo opened it, counted the contents to be sure it was all there, and pulled off three bills for Tony.

"I'm setting up another one for tomorrow," he informed Tony who was pocketing the bills. One of them would make him even more attractive at Lucinda's joint.

"O.K.," he replied. "Know where?"

"Nope."

"O.K., see ya'," Tony said as he turned and left.

Outside, he stopped a moment and looked over at the concentrating secretary, smiled, and invited, "Do you want to go out tonight?"

"I want," responded Thelma with a martyr's smile, "but I can't. Tonight's my night to sit with my aunt."

"I could come over there," Tony volunteered.

"Well, all right," Thelma responded. "But, it might not be any fun."

"We'll sing her to sleep," offered Tony.

After Tony left, Thelma smiled in anticipation. She would expect him around nine.

CHAPTER SEVEN

Meanwhile, halfway around the world in the faraway Philippine Islands, America's last bastion in the Pacific, the fat President was preparing for his grand tour of the United States. Some of his friends were preparing for something else.

General Augusto Ferreri (Donno to his friends) had a way with the heavy Philippine President. He had a way with the President's wife as well. He had sold them both on the value of an official visit to the United States.

With visions of high honors and good business deals, President Parquez had agreed to make the visit.

Madame, the President's wife, looked forward to an extensive shopping spree. Had she known its true extent in advance, she would have been shocked, concerned, and gratified.

The General turned to his fields, where he grew great quantities of poppies used in the manufacture of snow. He would make his already great fortune secure on this trip. Miami had been in contact and the deal was made Twelve million dollars would be paid to El General. Some of this, of course, he had to share with Madame Parquez.

One evening in a dark recess of the Presidential garden, during one of the President's many receptions, the two had met furtively. After a quick embrace, she made her point clear.

"Donno," she said in a business-like manner, "I have one-third. You want the ship to land in San Francisco, don't you?"

"What's mine is yours," the General gritted, not pleased with the high cost of this love affair. He needed her as a cover and she was taking full advantage of him.

"Thanks, Donno. You won't be sorry."

There was quiet talk going around about his succession to the Presidency upon the retirement of Parquez. She felt that her Donno's loyalty to the President should be repaid. He agreed.

They lingered another five minutes in the shadows and then returned to the brilliantly-lit ballroom. She entered through a French window on the terrace. He went around the building and came in through the main entrance.

The two main conspirators had agreed on the terms. All he had to do now was to refine the fruit of the poppy.

CHAPTER EIGHT

In muggy Tulsa, Marian's packing was nearly done. Three large and unstable suitcases held all of the clothing Mavis and Marian had, as well as most of Harold's finery. They also contained some toiletries and some lesser, frayed household linen and towels. Harold was left with a subsistence of minimal clothing and food to get him through the next week.

To get her out from underfoot, Marian sent Mavis to play with a little girl down the street. Marian had just finished tying a clothesline around the bag least liable to make the trip intact, when there was a knock at the kitchen door. She got up off the worn linoleum, put her scissors down, wiped the perspiration from the end of her nose, and went to unlatch the door.

A man stood there with a little case in his hand. He wasn't much to look at, but his green shirt and pants heralded some sort of official visit. Indeed it was. He had been sent by the landlord to check the air conditioner. There had been a complaint, he said.

"Air conditioner!" Marian laughed. "It's so old that it ought to be retired."

Then she looked again at the repairman and she recognized a pigeon. The man, in his early thirties, gave her a little smile and agreed that the machinery ought to be replaced.

"I was just making some iced tea," she said in a low voice. "Want some?"

"That'd be nice," the man continued to smile.

She noticed that his smile was warm. Indicating the living room door, she led him through the mess in the kitchen.

"Goin' someplace?" he asked.

"Yes, we're moving to San Francisco."

"Just my luck," he said, partly under his breath.

Although Marian was not unclothed, as she had been the day before, what she had on was designed for comfort on this sultry Tulsa afternoon.

"You wait here," she purred, as she pointed to the sofa. "I'll get the cold stuff."

He sat down. The sofa had seen better days and he sunk almost to floor level. Such a position provided for the informal.

Marian returned with a couple of glasses clinking with ice. She descended next to her guest.

Somehow, between putting the ice into the glasses and pouring the tea, she had managed to douse herself with a lilac perfume which would have made performing horses perform better.

Although the sofa had plenty of room on it for three persons comfortably and four in a pinch, Marian made it two in a pinch, notwithstanding the extra space available.

Although he was surprised, her green-suited guest offered no objection. He mumbled something about his gratitude for the drink. In response, she leaned back, and, in so doing, her flimsy dress fell away from her thigh. She made a feeble effort to cover herself, but failed.

Green-suit's eyes were on his poised glass, but not for long. He laughed nervously, and she rearranged her legs so that there was immediate proximity between the young man and herself. By this time, the poor fellow was experiencing his life flashing before him. But, these hasty reminiscences he put aside, along with his half-empty glass of tea. Marian had already disposed of her glass. He smiled. They said some things to each other, making little sense, something about how "they shouldn't." But, they did.

In a matter of seconds, Marian had enfolded her guest in her arms. Their lips met. Soon his tie fell to the ground and his shirt was opened to display a moderately hairy chest.

She whispered, "Let's go upstairs."

They did. Arm in arm. Clothing was dispensed with and the softness of the bed received them.

An acrobatic Marian gasped with pleasure and her guest echoed her feelings. This went on for some time until the physically-spent guest came to and thought of duty's call.

Ah, yes, the air conditioner. He slipped into his greens and became official. As he departed, all that Marian could think of was, "What a send-off!"

CHAPTER NINE

No one who has not experienced a move from Tulsa to San Francisco can understand the exaltation in Marian's heart as she left Harold at the departure door to board United Airline's flight #283 for the Golden Gate.

Harold had taken the late afternoon off to help Marian load the luggage. At the airport, he grudgingly paid for the extra weight.

Later, once the plane was aloft, as Mavis sat next to her in the crowded tourist section of the airplane, Marian thought back to her latest "experience" and tried to recall the air conditioner fellow's name. Then she realized that the physical exigencies of the moment had denied time for the social amenity of an introduction.

Marian and her daughter occupied two of the three seats available in row thirty-two. Mavis had the window seat. The aisle seat was occupied by John P. ("Call-me-Jack") Burwell.

Marian arranged matters for Mavis, then turned her attention to Mr. Burwell. He had thought he could concentrate on his paperback book, but found this hard to do, given the proximate chemistry of Marian. The lilac perfume helped a little, too.

"Where are you from?" inquired Marian.

"Well, I started in Wichita," Call-me-Jack drawled.

"Don't know anyone there," Marian said.

"Haven't missed much," Jack smiled.

"Live there now?" Marian was a prosecuting attorney.

"No, I live in St. Louis."

Marian had heard about St. Louis.

"Where are you folks going?" inquired the attentive Mr. Burwell. He looked over at Mavis and her coloring book.

"We're moving to San Francisco."

"Lucky."

"Yeah."

Somewhere in the chitchat, the sparks were exchanged and territorial barriers generally so natural in the three-seat configuration fell away.

Elbows touched. Jack asked if Marian was comfortable. She leaned in his direction.

Just then, the service cart worked its way into their aisle.

Why, yes, they would have drinks. She'd like a bourbon and ginger. Mavis would have a 7-Up. This she eventually spilled on the floor. No damage done.

Jack paid.

"What a nice man," Marian thought.

This observation really didn't say much for Jack, since Marian thought all men were nice.

Later, Jack divulged that he was going to San Francisco to establish an outlet for his carpet manufacturing company.

Marian, always thinking, saw her new floors covered with Call-me-Jack's highly discounted carpeting. Pretending to be slightly cramped, she lifted up the armrest between them and snuggled closer to the rug merchant.

They were soon flying through the darkness. Mavis had fallen asleep, covered by a blanket.

This left one blanket between Jack and Marian. Jack insisted that Marian make herself comfortable. Her little, white pillow was nestled against Jack's shoulder. Jack's arm and hand covered by the blanket had sought Marian's. A slight turn and their heads were quite close. Marian insisted that Jack share more of her blanket.

Soon a close friendship was made. With mutual good will, in the darkness of the speeding plane, each became familiar with the other.

To anyone who cared to look, an attentive husband was being attentive to his attractive wife. What an angel the little one was! Not a peep out of her as she hugged her dolly and saw to it that her thumb stayed in her little mouth.

Like daughter, like mother, only mother preferred Jack's warm and inviting lips to her own thumb. Her choice was roundly applauded by Jack, figuratively speaking, his hands being otherwise occupied.

And so, the trip to San Francisco whiled itself away. Call-me-Jack and Marian became good friends, one might even say bosom friends. The intimacy between them made the flight time pass. It also gave Jack a crick in the neck. Small payment.

The plane began its descent to the San Francisco Airport. Jack told Marian that he was staying at the Bedford Hotel. This is not the St. Francis or the Fairmont, but, since Marian knew neither of these two places, she remained impressed with the Bedford. The name had a nice, suggestive ring to it.

"My sister is meeting us," Marian informed Jack.

"I'll help you with your baggage," offered gallant and now-lost Jack.

He had been informed of the load in the baggage compartment stored for their arrival. They unraveled themselves from the informality of their improvised tent, checked seat belts, and awoke Mavis. The plane touched down, bounced once, and roared its reverse thrust as it sped down the lighted runway.

When they came into the passenger reception area, Leona detached herself from Ralph and the crowd, pushing forward to greet Marian and Mavis.

After much hugging and kissing, Leona picked up Mavis.

"My, you are a big girl, aren't you!"

Mavis agreed. "Where's Bubba?" she asked.

"He's at home. You'll see him in the morning."

She looked over at Ralph, wondering who he was. Jack had lingered in the background. Marian introduced him. Wonder of wonders, she had remembered his name. The real wonder was that she had ascertained this fact prior to the "experience."

Ralph eyed Marian, who had given him a little greeting kiss, and then he eyed Jack. Ralph had only the flimsiest of territorial claims. He and Marian once had shared the back seat of someone's car, until Leona had discovered them. But, that was a long time ago.

With clucking about how late it was and how sad it was that Leona had been put out, they all made their way to the baggage area. The crowd was already pushing in around the conveyor. Bags came, went, and were claimed.

At last, the clothesline-belted bag limped down the line. It was retrieved by Jack. Ralph had lifted an arm in preparation to lift it off, but Jack had beaten him to it.

All the bags but one had come through. Jack officiated each time. Then disaster struck. Ralph forced himself forward, elbowing Jack out of the way, and grabbed for the last bag. This was the one which Marian had felt was the most liable to make the trip without incident, so in it she had stowed her own effects—lingerie and personal toiletries. Just as Ralph gave the bag a tug, it fell apart. Actually, it disintegrated. The "one-horse-shay" of bagdom.

To Marian's horror, a collection too complicated and varied to describe fell out onto the moving conveyor belt. The "secrets" of the family were no longer secret. Ralph, with the bag handle in his hand, was catatonic.

Worse yet, as the humble belongings splayed themselves along the course of the conveyor belt, one item fell into public view which caused Marian to gasp. It was her tubular vibrator with its long electric cord.

Some people, once they had identified the object, had the bad manners to laugh out loud. Call-me-Jack, ever the gentleman, swooped it up and headed briskly to the door leading to the rear area of the baggage room. There, the conveyor belt made a turn in the long run through the loading dock.

As loading had been completed, no vehicles were there, but an operator was. He saw the de-bagged mélange coming toward him and he shut the conveyor down.

"Chrise," he exploded as if this had never happened before. "What a mess!"

He yelled to his assistant to get some cardboard boxes. Then he started to pick the items up. His were not loving hands. He crammed the bottles, toothbrushes, girdles, stockings, nightclothes, towels, shoes, hats, and all else into the odd-shaped cartons which airports keep for such purposes. Jack gallantly and surreptitiously pushed the vibrator into one of these.

The remnants of the old suitcase showed no sign of any possible usefulness. It was abandoned.

Jack rejoined the women. Ralph, having come to, had gone to get his Chevy.

At the curb, Jack helped them to wedge themselves in. Then he bade Marian goodbye, quietly suggesting that she call him at the Bedford. She said she would and she expressed her gratitude for his services. Her smile promised to express this gratitude in a more meaningful way later. Jack waved goodbye in a whirlwind of Chevy exhaust fumes.

Inside the crowded car, Ralph criticized the family's erstwhile savior.

"I wanted to pick up that bag myself . . . he pushed me," he explained. "That guy's a roughneck."

Marian defended Jack. "He was only trying to help."

"Naw, he was clumsy." Ralph was knowledgeable on that subject.

The car huffed its way from the airport through the freeways to Leona's house.

Since the garage was already full, Ralph thought it best to unload the car in the street in front of the house.

Piece by piece, with the help of the baby-sitter, each item made it to the living room.

"Better just leave this stuff here for the night," Leona suggested.

Marian had taken off her high-heeled shoes and was leaning against the doorjamb, holding them in her hand. The lighting, which was poor, gave the scene the look of a disaster shelter.

Ralph belched politely into the can of beer he had procured for himself.

"Want some?" he offered his sister-in-law.

By this time, Marian was so tired that this gallantry passed unnoticed.

"O.K., I'm going to bed," Ralph concluded.

Leona came over to Marian and said, "Come on, dear. Let's take Mavis up and I'll show you your room. I've given you the boys' room and let them camp out in the storage space."

"Oh, Leona, I've put you folks out," Marian purred. "Well, we won't be here long."

Mavis was put in a small bed and went right to sleep. Marian went back downstairs, riffled through one of the bags, and came up with her slippers. Her other things were unearthed from one of the airplane's cardboard boxes.

Back upstairs, she bumped into Ralph who graced his otherwise naked body with a towel.

"Putting on a little weight, there, aren't we Ralphie?"

"So what?" he rejoined and went into his room.

Marian kissed Leona good night, dumped her clothes on the floor, got into her nightgown, looked over at Mavis, and then tumbled into bed.

Wondering where the Hotel Bedford was, she gave two thoughts to Call-me-Jack, and fell fast asleep.

CHAPTER TEN

Morning dawned very early for Marian. She was on Tulsa time. Mavis, too. They arose and did their bathroom chores in relative peace and quiet.

At breakfast (an informal affair around the toaster), Leona said, "I'll call the real estate man and get the keys to the place."

"I can hardly wait," munched Marian.

And so, with Ralph eventually out of the way and the local clean-up accomplished, they set out with the children to walk to the real estate office and then they went over to the house.

They arrived at its portals about ten-thirty a.m. It was a typical side street house. Wooden steps led to a small porch. The place was in the last moments of a ten-year-old paint job. What had been cheery yellow at one time was now a peeling-off gray.

After surveying the house from the sidewalk, they climbed to the front door. The key fit and in they walked. Marian was conscious of a slight, musty smell of someone else's ménage. As they began to look around the living room, they sensed the noise of an electric appliance.

Leona's Bubba, with his five-year-old inquisitiveness, set out to find the source. As the place was not very big, he did not have very far to go. He pushed open the kitchen door, much to the surprise of a tall man who, up to that moment, had been shaving himself, gazing intently into the mirror over the sink.

"Hey!" the tall man yelled and, garbed only in his shorts, bounded into the living room.

Bubba beat a hasty and scared retreat to his mother's leg, which he grabbed and held onto for dear life.

The half-shaved inhabitant soon realized that he was in the company of two by now nearly hysterical women and what seemed like an army of crying children.

He was surrounded. Forgetting his disarray, he put up his hands in a gesture of peace at any price.

He was tall, and he was handsome.

Leona broke the impasse.

"We didn't know anyone was here," she croaked.

"Yeah, we rented the place," Marian gawked, not unaware that this fellow looked like a real hunk of a man.

"Yahhhh," yelled Bubba.

By this time, realizing that he was standing

there in front of two attractive women and as-
sorted children in his abbreviated apparel, he
retreated to the kitchen saying, "Hang on."

He grabbed his Hawaiian shirt, and pants, and
was in them very quickly. Then he returned.

"Now, what the hell is this?" he asked, his
voice booming through the crowded area.

"My sister is going to rent this place. We didn't
know anyone was here," Leona explained, now
that she, too, had regained control of herself.

The big man smiled at Leona. "Oh, that's
all right. Name's Tony. Going to rent the place,
huh? You'll like it. It's near the Park."

Leona pointed to Marian and said, "My sister
will be living here. I live several blocks away."

Marian came awake and said, "Yeah, we're
moving from Tulsa."

"Oklahoma?" queried an interested Tony.

"Right on," agreed Marian.

As there was nothing convenient to sit on, all
three continued to stand around what would have
otherwise been the living room.

"I'm moving to the YMCA," volunteered
Tony, "until I can find another pad."

He then offered to show the girls the extent
of the place. He was proud of the refrigerator.
It was only five years old.

"Sure, sure. Make yourself at home. My name
is Tony. Tony," he repeated. "If I can help,
just holler."

Before Marian had a chance to make use of Tony's introduction, Leona urged her to complete the tour.

After a quick survey of the upstairs, the troop left.

During the afternoon, while Leona was playing with the children in the backyard, Marian called the Bedford Hotel. The room clerk had never heard of John P. "Call-me-Jack" Burwell.

"The son-of-a-bitch," thought Marian and hung up. Well, she could invite help from Tony.

CHAPTER ELEVEN

The following day, after breakfast, Marian, dressed in blue jeans and a yellow sweater which left little to the imagination, returned to the house by herself, having left Mavis with Leona. This time, she rang the bell. When there was no response, she disappointedly opened the door with her key.

As she came in, Tony arrived from the other direction.

"Oh!" she cried. "I didn't expect to see you!"

"I was in the back, dumping junk into the trash barrel. Took a couple of days off," he explained, his open Hawaiian shirt displaying his strong chest.

Trying to look past him, she had to admit that the room did look a little tidier. However, the foam mattress was still in place and the radio was playing some rock base beat.

Marian wanted to go back upstairs, as she had not spent much time there during her last visit. Tony let her precede him up the stairs. Near the top, Marian appeared to miss a step and stumbled.

There may be some question as to whether she tripped, jumped, or was pushed, but the result that counted was the fact that she found herself in Tony's strong arms.

"I nearly fell!" she cried as he caught her. "Thanks a lot. I think I've hurt my ankle. I hope it's not sprained. Ooooh, damn it!"

"Don't worry, I'm here." And indeed he was. He held her in an iron grip, one arm strategically placed across her breast.

He took her back downstairs and placed her gently upon his informal couch. Marian faked pain, and Tony massaged the lower part of her leg.

Being experienced in these matters, and explaining that certain muscles in the upper leg should also be massaged to relieve tension, he proceeded with educated hands, as he suggested, to relieve the tension. Marian dissolved.

Soon, tension was being built up in areas which really had not suffered from the fall.

With her eyes almost closed, Marian gave a little sob and, with that, abandoned all pretense.

Like a tigress long parted from her mate, she leaped at Tony. Both rolled upon the mattress to which she had been carried. In this preliminary exchange, she and her yellow sweater parted company. Tony seized her and caressed her. That she responded was evident. Together they joined in Nature's race.

Tony was a tireless partner, effectively filling

his brief moments of respite with such legerdemain that voracious Marian scarcely noticed the difference.

One thing must be said for Marian. She demonstrated over and over that she was not a creature of habit or consistency in her choice of patterns followed to find and give release.

On his part, Tony had been kept fully occupied. For a man who obviously had such a variety of partners in the act, it is surprising that he should notice the originality of Marian's style and delivery. But, he did. He had to admit to himself, in his infrequent pauses, that Marian had the qualities of a kaleidoscope. No twist provided the same design.

Something new had been added for Mr. Tony.

The meanly-furnished living room, with its foam mattress, became a temple of love: carnal, basic, physical love.

In the heat and gymnastics of the encounter, neither gave thought to any plan for the rest of the day.

Marian's new living room had been really baptized. The shrine had been dedicated and she hoped that it would be visited frequently by believers. By this big believer, in particular.

Each morning for the rest of the week, she visited her new domain to "tidy up." Each visit ended in a wild celebration. An "experience." She forgot Call-me-Jack.

Tony smiled a wan smile when he said goodbye

to Marian and promised he would help her move when the time came. He was glad to get back to his undemanding garbage truck.

Marian wandered back down the street toward Leona's. For one of the few times in her life, she was hardly conscious of the admiring glances of male passersby.

When she got back to Leona's, the bad news was that Harold was on his way with the furniture.

But, there were other messages in other parts of town which had nothing to do with Harold.

CHAPTER TWELVE

Although the General had cautioned the President not to discuss his planned entry into the United States at San Francisco, he did. At the Corinthian-columned Bank of the Philippines, a building nestled into the Mongomery Street covey of foreign banks, young Fernando Loredo received a coded message:

"Uncle Charlie and Aunt Millie leave, stop. Show them the Bay and Alcatraz when they arrive."

Loredo re-read the message and wrote, "President plans to arrive San Francisco by ship."

"Good," thought Loredo. "We can get closer to them this way. The airport would be too damned fast."

He called his friend Miguel Calente and told him that Uncle Charlie was coming by ship.

"Great," said Miguel. "Guess we ought to start planning flowers."

Loredo laughed and added, "Guess he'll come in his own cruise ship. Anyway, we'll get the team together and we'll figure out what we can do to add to his welcome."

Even though the President's entry would be in broad daylight, Loredo was thinking of fireworks.

CHAPTER THIRTEEN

On Friday, skinny Harold showed up in a cheap U-Rent truck. He looked like a refugee from a Goodwill Center.

Harold was not an expert when it came to ropes, so he had used more footage than was needed. Not having placed the ropes judiciously, the furniture, boxes, sacks, and rugs had become an amorphous pile. The truck listed dangerously over the left rear wheel. However, it had made the trek, and now, outside of Ralph and Leona's, it sort of settled into the pavement like an old and tired horse.

Mavis ran out to kiss her Daddy and Marian followed. Just then Ralph limped up in the Chevy. There was a family reunion on the sidewalk. Leona thought Harold looked more relaxed than she remembered him to be. During this short respite without Marian to keep him jumping twenty-four hours a day, this was highly possible.

As it was late in the afternoon on Friday, they decided to leave the heap in the street for the night, and then on Saturday morning move it to its new resting place.

Marian, whose love for her furniture was born from familiarity, wondered if the chattels would be safe overnight.

Ralph took a look at the collection and worried to himself about what the street cleaning department might do with it. Otherwise, it would rest there unmolested except for the early morning fog.

As they all arrived with the listing U-Rent truck at the new quarters late the next morning, Tony came around the side of the house and greeted them.

"Welcome to your new home," he said to Harold with unusual friendliness, even before they had been introduced. Harold, though taken aback by this informal approach, nonetheless appreciated it. As it became obvious that Tony was there to help, he appreciated him even more.

Slowly, and with low groans from the relieved truck springs, the furniture was lifted to the front yard. Raven-haired Marian directed the traffic as it was carried into its new abode. Ralph, for once, was agreeable and even helpful.

Soon the house, so long without furniture, began to take on the aspect of a home.

Mavis' slide was put up in the backyard. Tony saw to that, winning Mavis' undying gratitude.

Marian and Tony, while placing furniture on

the second floor, had one or two moments of privacy in which to counsel with each other.

It was agreed that Tony would drop around in a day or two with a present for Mavis. By that time, Harold's schedule would be known and arrangements for future meetings could be established.

Tony almost offered to leave his telephone service connected, but, on wise second thought, did not make the offer. He thought it would inconvenience Marian to be interrupted by calls from his other girlfriends.

Harold reported to the U.P.S. office where he was expected. His shift was to be from four p.m. to midnight. There was no choice. He was just told. The U.P.S. center seemed much bigger to Harold than the one in Tulsa. Otherwise, much of the work would be the same.

CHAPTER FOURTEEN

Tuesday, Tony returned early to the garage, saying he needed to gas up for the rest of his run. Actually, one of his route customers had been awakened by a phone call from Rizzo to alert the driver to call in—it was urgent. He went straight up to Rizzo's office where he picked up a shoe box. Rizzo gave him an address. He was told that a suitcase would be given to him. The box was to be delivered in a new garbage can given to the subscriber to replace one which had been damaged by a company operator.

He headed his rig to the address.

A red-headed woman answered the door at Tony's ring.

"Thank you. You can leave the garbage can just inside the entrance here. My husband will put it out back." She paused and added, "Say, we were going to throw this suitcase away. Would you have any use for it?"

"Oh, thanks a lot. I'm moving into the YMCA and this is just what I need to carry my stuff. This'll work great."

He took the bag, somewhat surprised at its

weight, and placed it in his cab. He then returned to the plant, gave the truck to his friend, and took the bag with him.

"Hey, Tony, goin' somewhere?" asked the man.

"Yeah," said Tony, "after work."

"Lucky you."

"Yeah."

He went through the locker room and up the backstairs to Rizzo's office.

Rizzo leapt from his desk when Tony started into the office. He kicked the door closed with his heel and grabbed the suitcase just as Tony said, "Hey, Rizzo, the lady said I could keep the suitcase."

"Holy Moses," intoned Rizzo, as he felt the weight of the bag. "Hang on a moment," he added.

He dialed a number on his private line. After a short wait, he asked softly, "Shall I make a trip?"

There was no immediate response.

Then came, "I'll meet you in Marin at three."

"Tony is here. You want me to take care of him?"

"No. Have him drive you and I'll take care of both of you there."

"Will do."

Rizzo turned to Tony.

"Got your car?"

"Yeah "

"Get your lunch and meet me at two. You can take me to Marin, O.K.?"

"O.K."

It really wasn't O.K., since Tony had told Marian he'd be over during the afternoon, right after he had completed his route.

The trip to Marin led to what appeared to be an old boat house and building at an anchorage under the freeway. Its exterior had withstood the tides of time and the bay storms well enough to provide good cover for the clandestine meetings of Rizzo and Winship.

Rizzo left the car and was grudgingly handed the bag by Tony, who started to get out, too.

"You wait here, Tony," Rizzo ordered and he disappeared into a side entrance.

Within ten minutes, he returned smiling and gave Tony an envelope which included ten bills.

"Not bad." Rizzo had no trouble smiling as they headed back to San Francisco. "Now you can buy yourself a new bag, Tony," he laughed.

CHAPTER FIFTEEN

At the U.P.S. center, skinny Harold liked his new job. Working at night agreed with him. His tired look disappeared. He did not became loquacious, but his conversation was more lively than before. Maybe the climate effected the benefit. Maybe it was Marian. She was generally sound asleep when he came in around one a.m.

If she awoke at all, it was only to croak a hazy greeting and back to sleep she went.

Harold left well enough alone.

Their room at the back of the house had a view only of some fences and the neighboring gardens. Of course, coming in late at night as Harold did, what was in the garden neither disturbed nor elated him. He was a weekend gardener. The room's greatest asset was that it was quiet.

Unlike many who work at night, Harold was able to sleep through the morning hours without trouble. About one-thirty in the afternoon, he would rise and prepare himself for the day's occupation. He had a breakfast-lunch, which

Marian made for him. Then, off to the world of box-sorting.

Shortly after four, Tony would let himself in. Mavis greeted him as "Unca." He would spend a few moments admiring her dolly or making squiggles in her coloring book. Then she would go for her nap. Marian would take over. Occasionally Tony, at her direction, would help her with some household chore. They always ended up in bed.

Tony had attributes that Marian thought were beautiful. And he continued to seem tireless. For a big man, he was warm and kindly. His whole body made love. Even his marcelled hair.

In Marian, Tony had found a sister of Venus who was, in her ordinary way, a perfect animal. A trapeze performer! She had only to be touched to go into a frenzy of emotion. Her hands took over Tony and actually kneaded him as a sculptor would attack a mound of unmolded clay. This was accompanied by a series of happy and grateful squeals, cries, sighs, jumps, and groans. Tony, during these uncontrolled attacks, was not idle. His song of love was a stimulant to Marian such as she had not experienced before.

This particular day's idyll ended and Marian arose from her bed covered with perspiration which glistened in the fading sunlight.

Tony took this moment for a little concentrated rest. He fell fast asleep.

Marian eventually went to the kitchen and

prepared dinner for Mavis and Tony. It was a good dinner. Tony's "bills" had seen to that. Also, Marian's afternoon clothing, when she wore it, was cheerier and of better material than her early-in-the-day wardrobe.

"Tony, you shouldn't. You don't have to."

"Want to, baby, want to."

And his largesse seemed unending.

These trips to the garden did not happen every day. They did happen frequently enough, however, that Marian had to make up little stories for Leona which would discourage dropping in without calling first.

On the weekends, with Ralph and Harold, the sisters would take the children to the beach or the zoo or the Seal-Arama.

One day, in the middle of their first San Francisco November, Leona said to Marian, "Next week is Thanksgiving. We were going to Sacramento to be with Ralph's mother. I'd rather stay here with you. What do you think?"

"I think Harold wouldn't want to go to Sacramento," and they both laughed.

It was decided they would have a turkey at Leona's. Ralph figured he could get a good one at the Holiday Sureway, since his supervisors were offering an employee special.

Somewhere in the line of planning the day, Leona innocently suggested that maybe they should invite that Tony fellow who provided so much help when they moved in.

"He said he was going to live at the YMCA," Marian volunteered. "Maybe I can locate him."

"I hope so," Leona said. "He was a very nice man and I think he must be lonely."

Leona was not, in this instance, well informed. Marian repeated that she'd try to find Tony and invite him for the celebration.

The next afternoon, when she and Tony were together and during one of their breathing spells, they laughed out loud about "Tony's loneliness."

"Thanksgiving sounds good. Yeah, I'd like that," Tony accepted.

Thanksgiving day bloomed crisp and dry. This made the football players happy. It made the team owners even happier.

Ralph brought the turkey home. Leona prepared it, with Tony's help. It turned out that Tony's mother had been an excellent cook and had passed along her talents and recipes, hoping to make a chef out of her son.

Leona was very much impressed with this handsome man and his quiet assistance. Ralph and Harold paled by comparison.

The dinner eaten, the football game watched to the last field goal, the now-well-fed families and their friend bid goodbyes and went off to their various beds.

CHAPTER SIXTEEN

Early the next week, Leona planned to go downtown to do some shopping. Since Marian had offered to take care of the boys, Marian came over to pick them up. Shortly after Marian and the youngsters departed, the phone rang. It was Tony calling to thank Leona for including him at the Thanksgiving celebration. He asked her if he could drop by since he had forgotten his hat in the excitement. Although she had not seen it, Leona said, "Certainly."

Between the time Tony called and the time he arrived at the front door, which was just before lunchtime, Leona remembered a shelf in the upstairs hall she needed to have nailed up. Tony had been so helpful to Marian, maybe he would help her.

Help her he did. They stood side by side holding and hammering. Leona was up on a chair. After the job was done, Tony reached up to help her down. For one moment, they stood with their hands on each other. It was close enough so that an exchange was made.

Under normal circumstances, the job done, the

assistance rendered, the two should have parted. But, for one brief second, their eyes met and then their lips. Leona tried to pull back, but her effort was without will and before she knew it, she was in the game.

There was no effort to break the embrace before other notions could take place. One of Tony's large hands moved over Leona's back and hips while his other hand held one of her shoulders firmly in position. As she cradled against him, she felt him come alive. They kissed as though they had known each other for a lifetime. He sought her depths and hungrily she fell into his.

Each knew that a great moment in their lives was at hand: Tony out of habit and Leona from need. He leaned over and kissed her again and again. She surrendered completely, willingly, urgently.

Each had realization of what the immediate future had in store. Tony leaned in the direction of the bedroom. Leona followed. Kissing him, she turned awkwardly to undo her clothing. Realizing the street was in full view, she paused long enough to adjust the shade. Then she let her skirt and blouse slip to the floor. Tony fumbled familiarly with the clasp of her bra. It came apart and the bra fell to the floor with the other things.

Leona was inwardly surprised at the effortless speed with which the events were transpiring without any seeming physical assistance from her.

Nature was leading the parade. The new-found lovers had only to follow.

Tony drew her gently to him and let his hand drop along the line of her hip and then to the center of all her feelings. With a deftness which the gift of experience had given him, Tony dropped his clothing to find hers.

There is one swift moment between male and female when Nature requires a visual appreciation between the two that indeed each is of a different sex. Tony's excited documentation was devoured with a swelling warmth within Leona that left no doubt that each was as they purported to be.

The soft pressure of Tony's hand in its rhythmic embrace as they stood together in their first moment of real consent so pulsated through the being of Leona that with closed eyes she cried out for the moment to last forever.

This was no new moment for Tony and yet, deep within him as he looked down at the vision he held, he became grateful. At first, as gratitude was a stranger to his way, he did not recognize its symptoms.

They kissed deeply and he led her where they both could share the mystery that Nature had prepared for them.

She surrendered herself to him completely. Together they sought the softness of her bed.

Leona was alive again. Wanted and serving. What life, what warmth, what completeness! No fanfare, no gymnastics, yet everything playing, feeling, offering, taking, and then the great moment of oneness. Ten thousand stars lighted the night of her life.

Later, as they disentangled themselves, Leona had no feeling of remorse. Only the joy of discovery. No concern of conscience, only a reawakening for which she was deeply thankful. As she left the bed, her toe struck a shoe which Ralph had carelessly left beside it. She leaned over, grabbed the offending item, and hurled it into the hallway. So much for Ralph.

When they dressed, they kissed goodbye and promised each other a second meeting.

The woman in Leona was about to be saved.

CHAPTER SEVENTEEN

Tony, that night at dinner with Marian, thanked *her* for a happy Thanksgiving. Marian, with a big kiss, thanked Tony for making it so much fun.

"Honey," Tony said softly, "any chance of you getting away some night to go dancing with me?"

"Not too easy, Tony. How we gonna get a sitter to stay with Mavis without someone finding out?"

"Easy. We just get back before eleven-thirty and I take the sitter home. Easy."

"O.K., if you think we can make it work. I'll look around for a sitter."

"Now, here are a couple of 'bills.' Get yourself some dancing shoes and a goin'-out dress."

"If you insist, you nice guy."

"Just want you to be happy."

"Don't worry."

And the dancing life of Marian was being arranged.

Tony got around so much during the day that a nighttime regime including dancing would have seemed impossible had it been anyone else. But, Tony was Tony. The wellspring of strength.

The first place he took her to was a Latino spot in the Mission District. Marian was not a good dancer, but it didn't matter. Tony led her through the steps without noticeable mishap. About eleven-fifteen, they realized that the pumpkin was about to arrive and they scurried home.

A quick kiss at the door, and the sitter bustled off with Tony. She was paid on the way to her house.

Marian ran upstairs, jumped out of her goodies, which she hung up neatly in a little closet to which she alone had the key. By twelve-fifteen, she was in bed.

She was in the middle of a wild fandango when she heard Harold close the front door.

Harold! What did he know? The alphabet, the zip code, the difference between "K" and "L" or 94ll8 or 50426.

The fandango stopped as Harold arrived at the bed in a haze of alcohol. He had been drinking!

He slithered out of his clothes, put his glasses on the dresser, and went into the bathroom where he gargled loudly. Then he returned in his pajama top. Up to this point, Marian pretended to be asleep. Upon seeing the pajama top through her half-closed eyes, she gasped, "Harold?"

"Who else?" quipped Harold, carried away by his gin and ginger.

With a deft action, he slipped under the connubial covers. Marian felt his skinny, chilly hand on her backside.

"Your hand is cold, Harold."

"Won't be long."

"Don't, Harold. I have a headache and I have just gotten to sleep."

"I'll fix the headache," he challenged, and lunged for her.

Marian, tired from dancing the cha-cha-cha, made a feeble attempt to throw him off. He pinned her, as was his right he thought.

What happened then was such a charade, such a mockery of the beauty to which Marian was now accustomed, that she stifled a laugh and pretended to be coughing. Her "cough" erupted just at the moment Harold was on the point of a weak penetration, so that her pelvic jerks released on contact what little Harold had to give. It was enough for him, though. He retreated, satiated, and, with little thought of his wife's comfort, turned over and fell asleep.

Marian began to plan her escape.

Help was on its way.

CHAPTER EIGHTEEN

The Miami group had, in addition to its North American sources, recently developed contacts with the Philippine paradise and this contact was about to pay off.

Rizzo's little-used boathouse and harbor on San Francisco Bay would provide facilities to receive and distribute the shipment.

Winship was sold on the benefits of this port. It was a safe meeting place, away from the hurly-burly of City Hall and its large ears.

At one time, the place had been a relatively successful marina. It was now old-fashioned and there was no room to expand. The facilities had fallen into disrepair. A couple of older boats were beached. One lay out in the water and the water lay in it. At high tide, the roof of the pilot cabin was all that was visible. It listed drunkenly to one side.

Former tenants had moved to San Rafael's classy new marina.

The old channel, however, due to fast tidal action, remained deep and navigable.

The interior of the old boathouse had been

renovated, providing a good-sized apartment on top, with a balustraded deck. The bedroom overlooked a wide expanse of Bay. It had a mirrored ceiling and a comfortable and not-too-large Jacuzzi hot tub. Food and drink were in good supply. In this surrounding, failure to provide peacock feathers went unnoticed. Sometimes Rizzo visited the spot with some unsuspecting bimbo.

It was possible, from this port, to disappear into four or five directions. A fast boat could go up the river or out of the Golden Gate. Cars could easily speed north, or across the Richmond Bridge to the east. The Golden Gate Bridge could handle the southern deliveries. Most importantly, a little to the north there was a private airport.

Shipments of snow could be transferred to a speedy whaler in the cover of Bolinas Bay near Stinson Beach.

Recently, Rizzo had taken a Miami contact to the marina boathouse in the company of a well-endowed young dictionary designer. Pretending to have forgotten an appointment which would take him at least two hours, he left the happy couple. Later, he called to find out how things were going with his Florida friend. All went so well for "Florida" that he was giving serious consideration to moving West. As this would inconvenience the business operations, he did the next best thing. He invited his curvaceous partner to return to Florida with him.

By the time Rizzo showed up, the girl was affecting a southern accent.

Fun aside, "Florida" had seen the strategic importance of the location and Rizzo was given the order to ready it for the Philippine goodies.

CHAPTER NINETEEN

The next afternoon, shortly after four, Tony waltzed into Marian's house. He gave Mavis a pat on the head and her mother a pat on her tightly-fitted posterior. Mavis left for her little friend's house, with enough money to go to a movie. Tony, seeming pensive, went and sat on the plush couch.

"Baby," he said, looking over at a derailed Marian who had her foot on the staircase, "we got some guests comin' to town and they want to go dancing."

"So?" said Marian, coming into the living room.

"Yeah," he continued, "they'll be here in a couple of days. My boss thought we'd have a party."

"Harold would like that," joked Marian, who was already planning her wardrobe for the gala evening.

"He's not invited." Tony was serious.

"Of course not," she said.

"Rizzo asked me to find a girl for him who would put out and who would be fun."

"Sounds great! How about Leona?"

"Oh, uh . . . I don't think so. Anyway, we'll probably need her to take care of Mavis."

"Yeah, I guess so . . ."

"I'll work something out."

"When will this happen?" Marian did not want to be caught unawares.

"They'll be here next weekend."

"Well," she mused, "I can tell Harold I need a rest. I really do. Take Mavis to Leona's and then I'll go away some place. I heard Santa Rosa's nice. Guess you can get there by bus easy enough."

"What do you want to go to Santa Rosa for?" Tony was slow catching on. "Oh, sure, I see. You tell him that's where you are going to go. That's great."

"Something like that."

"You're on then?"

"Sure, Tony. Anything for you."

They talked over the plan, time, places, what to wear and what not to wear, and then Nature led them into what was becoming a delightful habit.

Tony left Marian enough money so she could buy the necessaries. Amongst other things, she would make a thing about buying a bus ticket. She would arrange the motel accommodations by phone within earshot of Leona. The plan would work. Harold could eat cat food for the weekend.

As Tony left around eleven, Marian looked him over and began figuring out what kind of husband he'd make.

CHAPTER TWENTY

"Marian's coming over," Leona shared with Tony at luncheon. "She'll be here around three. She's bushed. The move and all . . . and wants to take a little vacation in Santa Rosa. I'm going to help her plan her trip."

"You're a great sister to have," sang Tony.

"Well, she doesn't have a very exciting life with Harold. Oh, he's all right, I guess, but I don't know if I could take him for long. Anyway, it doesn't seem to bother Marian. I don't know how she does it."

Tony blinked his eyes and nearly said, "Beautifully."

"Yes, Tony. She needs a little vacation, if only for a weekend. Mavis can come here. We'll have fun."

With that, she came over and kissed Tony.

"Yeah, fun," she said.

And that is just what they had until Tony left shortly before three.

It should be said that housekeeping each day in the Remmer household was done in record time. No sooner was Ralph out of the door than things were zip, zip, zip. Kitchen cleaned, upstairs put together, the comfy bedclothing Tony had given her the money to buy put in place, the bathroom sparkling, children clean, clothes washed, dusting done. Not much time left for whistling. Then, the neighborhood playschool for the kids.

When Tony arrived at eleven, everything was ready for him, just as if he was returning to his own home.

Although these visits did not happen every day, they were happening frequently enough so that Leona had little stories to tell Marian which would discourage random visits.

For Tony, it was, most times, luncheon with Leona and dinner with Marian.

So far, no problem.

Now, as Leona put her arm around Tony's waist to lead him on a path she well knew, she warmed inside and thought how marvelous it would be if Ralph could take a leaf from Tony's book. Later, she began to think of no Ralph at all. Her pulse skipped a beat or two

Leona rejoiced in her good fortune which made her other tribulations seem bearable. Then she sank into her wonderful world with Tony and came alive.

She didn't worry over pregnancy. The outpourings of Ralph she could control. This man Tony was something different. With him, although she always did what she should, she

didn't let fear stand in the way of their completeness. When all was done and her saddest
moment was upon her—the parting—she
asked him if he could arrange to go to the park
on Saturday.

"Aw, I'd love that," said Tony, forcing it a
little, "but I have to do some overtime for my
boss this weekend."

Leona was disappointed. "There'll be another
time."

Tony whispered, "I'm glad of that."

As it turned out, Ralph went bowling on Saturday and Leona took the kids to the park herself.
She was just as happy. They found the merry-
go-round.

CHAPTER TWENTY ONE

Harold was put out that for two days he would have to take care of himself. By the same token, he did not begrudge himself a weekend alone. Marian didn't add much anyway.

Early Saturday morning, Harold had driven her to the bus station in his banged-up second-hand car. Half the time, the thing wouldn't work, but this time it did. As Harold left, Tony, who had been waiting, embraced Marian as if she had just arrived on Greyhound bus #36 from Fresno, although she looked better than that.

For the occasion, Tony had booked a room at the Hotel Bedford. When Marian saw the place, the name registered slowly, and then she remembered "Call-me-Jack." That son of a bitch! Well, she'd make up for it this weekend.

Up in their home-away-from-home, she hung out her clothing and established her beachhead in the small bathroom.

She called the Santa Rosa motel and cancelled,

saying the arrival of a friend from out of town made it necessary to change plans. She was now ready for whatever the next two days would serve up.

CHAPTER TWENTY TWO

Sometime after five o'clock on Saturday afternoon, Marian and Tony were lolling in that wonderful in-between when the phone rang. It was Rizzo.

"O.K., Tony, you got it set?"

"Yeah, yeah," said Tony. "I'm waiting for a call."

"Better be good," said Rizzo.

"Take it from me, boss!"

"O.K., let's meet at the dock around nine."

"Got it."

He hung up, and, just as he did so, the phone rang again.

"Tony?"

"Hi, Millie. Come on up. Four twenty-two."

"Come on up?" yelled Marian. "What the hell does that mean?"

"Millie Du Pris is coming up. She's going with us tonight. She's for Rizzo."

"I'm not dressed!"

"You look great."

"Tony, what is this?"

A loud knock at the door. Tony hopped out of bed.

He had the door open before Marian could object. What came through the door was all ready to go to the party.

Her hair had really been "done." Her costume was an advertisement. Her nails and lips matched, and her eyelashes looked like harvest rakes.

Marian held the coverlet over her breasts and could hardly believe what Tony was doing. He had grabbed Miss Phone and Knock and was giving her a big kiss, which the lady was receiving with her hand cupped beneath Tony's equipment.

"Didn't want to hurt anything, honey," she gushed as she came away from him.

Spying Marian, she exclaimed, "Oh, hello, you lucky gal!"

All Marian could say was, "Pleased to meet'cha."

And Tony jumped back into bed.

"Thanks for filling in at the last minute, Millie," Tony smiled.

"No trouble. Call me anytime."

She sat down in the only armchair in the room and with a deft motion, she took her shoes off. She started to light a cigarette.

"Oh, excuse me. Is it all right if I smoke?"

"If you don't mind getting it in your hair." Marian was not being very nice

"Guess that's right," Millie said, looking around. "What's the matter, Tony? Couldn't you get a double room? This place is a cage."

Judging by what was going on it, she wasn't far wrong.

After the shock had worn off, Marian paraded from the bed to the bathroom, where she put on her robe. Millie had seen enough to understand Tony's point of view.

Tony's nonchalance with this "intruder" got to Marian. While she was straightening out her hair, with bobby pins clenched between her teeth, she was trying to figure out what she should say and do next.

Getting mad at a man like Tony could have bad consequences. He could walk out. Marian didn't want that to happen. At the same time, she was miffed and a little jealous of the freedom with which Millie had walked into her life.

She put on her mascara. The concentration needed for that effort quieted her feelings of mayhem.

By the time she returned to the small bedroom, she was composed and smiling.

As she entered she noticed that Tony had on his shorts and that Millie was laughing uproariously at something he had said.

In his mind, Tony had given some consideration to inviting Millie to join him with Marian in bed. He then realized that the girls really didn't know each other that well Also, Millie had her hair cemented together to last through the evening's festivities.

She was laughing because Tony had apologized for not offering more in the line of early evening entertainment.

Millie tried to explain the levity. Marian did not find it so amusing. But she had told herself in the bathroom mirror that she would keep her cool.

"What's the plan, Tony?" Millie wanted to get the program straight.

"We'll meet Rizzo about nine. Good dancing, good eats, lots to drink. You'll have a great time. Some of his pals from out of town will be there."

"Hey, wait a minute, Tony. I'm not going to get into any gang deal."

Marian just watched.

"Don't worry, Millie. Marian and I'll be there. These are swell people. You'll like them. Guess they're rich, too."

"O.K., but not kinky-pinky or I'll yell and leave."

Marian noticed by the t.v. time signal that it was seven-thirty.

"We'd better get ready, don't you think?" And she made a move to the closet where her goodies were hanging.

"Yeah, guess so," agreed Tony. "I'll shave quick."

"You do that," chimed in Millie. She turned

up the t.v. while the dressing procedures took place.

Marian accomplished what she could in the small closet and came over to Millie.

"Zip me up, honey, will'ya?"

"Sure."

Wasn't much to zip, and Marian looked like she had stepped out of a Macy's catalogue. Her dress wasn't great, but she was. Even Millie gave her an admiring glance.

Tony finally completed himself in a ruffled blue shirt and a large bow tie. He wore a white coat. He had rented the outfit.

With a last look at themselves in the mirror on the dresser, they went down into the hotel lobby. Since Tony had parked his car nearby, they walked there together.

CHAPTER TWENTY THREE

Tony drove through the evening traffic toward Fisherman's Wharf, cutting to the right on Bay Street just before the Wharf business area began. He drove along the Embarcadero, made a U-turn, and parked in front of a warehouse marked Pier 32.

Marian looked around. The place was badly lighted. Tony led them through a narrow passageway along the side of the building. They were going onto a ship. Its hulk loomed high in the shadows of the night.

A brawny fellow came out from behind a shed and asked who they were coming to see.

"George Rizzo," answered Tony.

"Go up the gangplank, where the light is, and walk to the stern. It's the first starboard door."

Millie gave the fellow the once over and crooned from the old song, "They knew he was a sailor 'cause he wore a sailor hat . . ."

They crossed the gangplank and walked to the stern where they found a brass-bound door under a deck light.

Millie opened the door, since Tony was bringing up the rear. As she did so, the deck came ablaze with light, and they entered what in Navy language looked like a ward room. A gussied-up one.

Rizzo was with two women, noticeably taller than he, and he was in conversation with two well-dressed men, one older than the other.

Rizzo turned and eyed the women who had just entered. He and his cigar came forward.

"O.K., Tony! O.K.!" he admired.

"George, this is Marian and this is Millie. Millie is for you. Girls, meet George Rizzo."

Rizzo put out his brown and hairy hand.

"Welcome aboard, honey. And, you too, dear." He was oily.

He gave his other hand to Millie.

It was Millie's turn. "Pleased to meet'cha," she smiled.

"Hey, fellas, say hello to Marian and . . ."

"Millie."

"Yeah, say hello to Millie."

Marian was just getting over the bright lights.

Now these fellows were as different from Tony and Rizzo as night is from day. They were not flashy. They looked like successful and conservative businessmen, except for their jewelry, which was more noticeable than they were.

"Harry, this is Marian," Rizzo repeated, taking her by the arm to where Harry was. Harry's smile was professional.

Over his shoulder, Rizzo introduced her. "Millie, say hello to Mr. Murphy."

"Hello, Mr. Murphy," Millie said in her way to make people sit up and take notice. "Say, we've got the market on good looks, haven't we?"

Mr. Murphy, older than the others, was obviously pleased. He agreed completely with Millie.

Murphy looked like a cross between a tall priest and an aging college professor. He was balding and what hair he had was gray. He was certainly courtly, almost of the old school. He had a heavy, not to say, commanding, voice. But, he spoke quietly like one whose security is assured.

He turned to introduce the other women. One was Midge and the other was Mrs. Murphy. Mr. Murphy's wife looked as though she had married him recently. Any less recently and she would have been thirteen years old, which was against the law.

Then Mr. Murphy expanded, "What will you have?" and the evening was off.

Just at that moment, some large ship passed close by and its wake made the ward room roll.

"Hey-ay," yelled Millie. "I think I've already had it!" And everybody laughed.

The younger man told Rizzo that the Captain could shove off.

"Not yet. Winship's coming," Rizzo apologized.

"Well, let's get with it."

As if on cue, the ward room door opened again and in stepped Winship. In her evening slacks, she was masculine and beautiful at the same time.

"Hi, group. Hope I'm not late," was her throaty greeting.

"Never too late," smiled Rizzo and he began showing her around.

Tony, in his limited mind, was trying to put matters together. He had always thought that Winship was a man. Her tone of voice indicated to him that he wasn't altogether wrong.

Mr. Murphy took Rizzo's arm. "I believe that we may leave now, Mr. Rizzo."

Rizzo left to give the Captain the order. Marian sensed that the room vibrated, and no sooner had Rizzo returned than the vibration became a heavy hum. Marian was conscious of movement. The ship was underway. Drinks were served.

Millie attached herself to George Rizzo.

"C'mon, big boy," Millie breathed to Rizzo. "Take me out on deck. I wanna see the lights."

There was a big sweater on a chair and this she put over her shoulders. Rizzo put down his cigar to help adjust it for her.

This duty performed, he opened the door and stepped through, expecting Millie to follow. She did.

There was a stiff, fresh breeze. The Bay Bridge seemed overhead. The lights of Oakland shown like jewels in the distance. Rizzo steered Millie across the fantail deck to a couch which formed the stern and they sat down together. Rizzo was not interested in the distant scenery. He was a close-up type. He held onto Millie's arm. She pretended not to notice and, using her free hand, sipped the fizzy drink someone had given her.

"George, if I may call you George, Mr. Rizzo? Isn't it beautiful?"

"Yeah, with a capital B," he agreed.

She was having a hard time getting her fizz to her lips since George, small though he was, had shifted position so as to place his face directly in the way.

She looked at him closely. She had to. She noticed he had hairs growing out of the pores of his nose.

"Millie!" she yelled at herself silently. "What the hell's the matter with you? You got a nice date and you're looking at his pores already."

"Oh, George," she breathed heavily, hoping that Rizzo had not sensed her observation.

George was close enough now so that she could smell his earlier drinking pattern.

"Wanna share a joint, honey?" His eyes were lighted by the starboard light. A nice green.

"Let's wait until later, Georgie," Millie said, not moving her head. Instead, with her hand carefully holding her fizz glass, she circled his neck and pulled him toward her. She gave him a great big, friendly kiss.

George Rizzo, used to the begrudged attentions

of Thelma, the woman who worked for him, was overcome. He mistook a friendly little kiss of introduction as an invitation to come aboard. As his hands went into action, Millie was taken aback. However, she managed the situation.

"You funny guy, you got me started," and she nuzzled him.

"Millie," he croaked. "Millie."

"Yes, George?"

"You do things to me."

"George, you do them to yourself."

"When I first saw you," he slurred, "that's for me, I said."

"That's funny, George. I said the same thing. But, Georgie, it's cold out here. I'm your girl, Georgie, I'm your girl." And with that she let George have it and nearly smothered him.

She rose, not with elegance, but with what balance the boat's motion and her gin intake permitted, and walked indirectly to the door.

She looked over her shoulder. George was rising unsteadily with a silly grin on his face.

He wheezed, "O.K., baby. Later." Then he opened the door with the exaggerated politeness which comes with anticipation and incipient drunkenness. Millie passed through.

Mr. Murphy was telling some sort of story, and the others were laughing. Mrs. Murphy was sitting on Mr. Murphy's knee like a pretty little ventriloquist's doll. The lights of the city were fading into the distance and the ship had taken on a steady roll. They were crossing in front of the Golden Gate.

At one of the bulkhead walls, Harry was trying to explain some detail in a framed photograph to his friend Midge, who kept getting closer and closer to the picture, until the boat gave a mild pitch. And both of them slid down the wall to the floor behind a large armchair. They were oblivious of any audience. It was clear that they liked each other.

Marian, whose life had not included gatherings of this nature, was trying to cope with this new-found sociability.

The cabin attendant, a Navy type, entered and told Rizzo that dinner was served in the Mess.

With some straightening of hair and adjustment of skirts, the ladies preceded the men into a cozy, nautical dining room.

Winship had taken a shine to Tony, which miffed Marian. However, having lived through the events of the afternnon, Marian was ready for almost anything.

The dinner passed very well. Fine foods, good, but completely unappreciated, wine, and a fine French dessert. Table conversation of a low order. Then the smoking started. Fine Mexican grass. Neither Marian nor Tony smoked. Millie did and soon disappeared with Rizzo to one of the sumptuous guest cabins.

CHAPTER TWENTY FOUR

Mr. Murphy unlocked the cabin door and stood back to let Winship pass through.

He carefully locked the door and turned up the piped-in music.

Winship turned to him. "All right, Mr. Murphy, what's up?"

"A great deal is up."

"Tell me."

"Well, first of all, I have something for you," he said quietly and reached under the large bed to pull out a hand-tooled briefcase.

"Nice leather," she remarked.

Mr. Murphy passed his hand over it and said, "Well, the case is nice. What's inside is nicer."

He opened the case. Several envelopes could be seen. He chose one and gave it to Clarissa Winship. Like a cat, her dark eyes followed him.

When it was firmly in her hand, she opened it. It was a fat $150,000.00.

"We appreciate," from Mr. Murphy.

"I can see," the Mayor's helper gasped.

"We like the way that your 'educational'

department is doing. We like your 'defense' department, too."

"I wondered if anyone noticed."

"We did, and someday we want to meet the gentlemen who set up those schools. We're having trouble in Portland and Seattle."

"Really? Our kids love the stuff. They've become attached."

"Good, good."

"Well, maybe not good, but profitable. The dumbheads won't amount to much, anyway."

"Are you servicing the private schools?"

"Are you kidding? Lots of money. School lunches cost more now, you know!"

She laughed and held the envelope close to one of her almost nonexistent breasts.

Murphy laughed along with her. "Winship, you're great."

"I hope."

"You have one of the biggest territories, you know. We want you to be happy."

"I'm happy, I'm happy!" laughed Clarissa Winship, patting herself with the envelope so that her other breast could have its share of pleasure.

"And now for the important business of the evening." Mr. Murphy's brow furrowed.

Clarissa leaned forward. She was sitting in one of the master cabin's big chairs.

"Yes?" she concentrated.

"We thought that the next shipment was on its way from Peru, but someone sliced it and it's not coming through."

"I'm sorry."

"Well, it's not all that bad. I think something better is happening. We have had for sometime a Philippine contact which we feel now is going to really pay off. They just have to keep President Parquez there for another month."

"I heard he was part of it."

"His opposition is spreading that as a rumor. His lead General runs the show."

"Then what's the problem?"

"The President's wife seems to have some idea as to what's happening and she wants in."

"Give it to her." Winship, the women's rights advocate.

"Easily said. Her pal, the General, is very much concerned that if he brings her in right now, she will upset the program. He said she talks too much, and the last time she had some heavy cash, she went on a shopping spree that nearly sank the President in the last election."

"Some gal!" Clarissa thought she recognized class.

"Well, she's a problem." Mr. Murphy was concerned.

"Have we done business with this outfit before?" asked Winship.

"Well, we've done business, but on a much smaller scale. Sometimes very erratic."

"From what you say, it seems they're better organized now."

"It is better organized, because now the President is part of it whether he knows it or not. We don't want to upset anything."

"What can I do?"

"Clarissa, I thought you'd never ask!"

"Well, I have."

She re-crossed her legs slowly. Mr. Murphy pretended to take no notice, but he did, and lost a few pulse beats in the effort.

"We must plan a celebration for the President," he said.

"Aren't we?"

"Be serious, Clarissa."

"Well . . ."

"A celebration. A parade. Like you folks in San Francisco do so well, except that this one has to be in the water."

"The water?"

"Yes."

"So?"

"Fire boats, salutes, yachts, sailboats, wind surfers, all sorts of excitement."

"Are you expecting Queen Elizabeth?"

"You're getting the picture."

"You do or you don't?"

"Don't. But we do have President Parquez."

"Holy cow," she said with some sarcasm

"Better. It's his first, and probably last, official visit to the United States. Through the Golden Gate and on to Washington. He wants to stay in the United States."

"There goes our source."

"No one knows that yet."

"You do."

"Well, let's say that our friends know and that's why they want to take full advantage of the visit. We want to be sure to get on with the new people."

"So I suppose you want big things from the Mayor?"

"Just a lot of noise."

"Excitement?"

"Yes, excitement. We'll take care of the rest."

"I see."

"I hope so. Can you arrange fire boats, a fifty-gun salute from the Presidio, the works?"

"Yes, but only twenty-one guns for a Chief of State at the Presidio."

"If it's noisy, that will be enough."

"What's your idea?"

"Well, I want a lot of jumping around." Mr. Murphy's arms and hands designated the all encompassing. "It will help us with the pick-up."

"Oh, we can have so much going on that I don't think anyone will spot us."

"That's what we need for cover."

Clarissa was satisfied that the job could be done.

"Once you have the stuff, where will you go?"

"The plan is to head for the old marina Rizzo has found for us."

"Well, I'm glad that's arranged."

"So am I."

Mr. Murphy smiled over at Clarissa.

"Don't you worry, Mr. Murphy. We'll have so many boats and so much noise that no one will have time to do anything but try to navigate."

"I knew you'd understand."

"I'll make sure the Mayor understands, too. He's a nut for regattas."

And so with the conference accomplished, the payoff for services rendered, and the plan laid out for services yet to come, Clarissa rose and shook hands with Mr. Murphy. His were clammy. Hers were as cold as ice.

He replaced the tooled leather briefcase under the bed and led the way from the master suite, carefully locking the door behind him.

CHAPTER TWENTY FIVE

Marian had enjoyed her dinner. Harry was her dinner partner on one side and Tony was on the other.

After dinner, she and Tony went on deck. She wrapped herself in the sweater Millie had discarded after her waltz with Rizzo.

With this crew, Tony looked out of place. Somehow, it had gotten through to him. He was defensive.

Marian sensed his discomfiture and pulled him onto the fantail couch.

"Tony, sweetie, I love you." She nuzzled him, hoping to get his ego back in place. "I'd take one of you to any twenty of them." And she jerked her head toward the ward room.

He looked over at her gratefully, his eyes so sad that Marian took him into her arms and caressed his marcelled hair.

"You're good, Marian," he sobbed. He had been drinking and his sob was part of his effort to catch his breath. They kissed each other for as long as it took to brighten Tony's outlook.

He was afraid Marian might find him shabby in the bright light of these other people.

Marian let him know differently. She really loved this side of him, and the tenderness with which she mended him said it softly and beautifully. Tony just lay there, content for once to be the lover loved, not the hunter in pursuit. His ear brushed her radiant lips and, changing positions, she whispered, "Tony?"

"Yes?"

"Do you love me, Tony?"

"Marian, baby, who else?"

She was about to divulge to him her plan of escape.

Suddenly, he sat upright, without warning, and looked at her as she reclined in the wavering light at the stern of the yacht.

"Baby, I'm not much. I can't say what I want to. You're so beautiful." All this expelled in one breath.

"Oh, Tony, love."

"Please, honey, I've been trying to say something. Something I've never said to any broad before."

"Go ahead, Tony. I'm not a broad, but go ahead."

(No broad thinks she's a broad.)

Tony, moved by the softness he saw reflected in the starlight, found reaction to the irresistible preferrable to words. Marian opened her arms, closed her eyes, and breathed her invitation. So immersed were the two of them in their pursuit, that what happened next did not immediately intrude itself.

Millie fell through the door along with the blazing light and the distant blare of disco music.

"C'mon, Georgie, up for a little air."

She was in disarray, really. George was flying.

"Hey, babe. You broke up something beautiful in there."

"No, no, I didn't. I just didn't want to suffocate. You're so strong, Georgie."

The cabin door closed. In the darkness, the presence of the music was still felt.

George tried to straighten out his clothing. His coat was not so bad, but his trousers were open where society decrees they should be closed. George was in hot pursuit. He made an awkward pass at Millie, who playfully ducked behind a low table. But, not fast enough. George's shin made full contact with a chair leg and, as she turned to save him, they both were decked, rolling and laughing on the heavy carpet. Of course, they had not seen Tony and Marian in the shadows of the stern. They fell onto each other like a couple of panting animals.

Millie's gown, such as it was, had fallen from her shoulders. Since she wore no bra, her ample breasts were free in the salt air. The cool of the night, to say nothing of the state of excitement, had made stiff little minarets of her nipples.

In falling, George, with one major swoop of

his hand, had rearranged Millie's skirt so that what had dropped from the top and was scooped up from the bottom resembled a gaudy-colored life preserver around her middle. George had freed himself of the normal restrictions of his trousers and had come to rest on the cloying Millie. Knees up, head back, arms clutching, she was his. The effort of the world delivered his message.

Marian took all of this in over Tony's shoulder.

Although he heard the music, he was not conscious of the activity, since his back was to the action, and his attention, mind, and hands were on Marian.

The antics of Millie and her drunken companion, instead of cooling Marian, only served to heighten her excitement. Conscious that Tony was losing his own control, she regarded the others with an air of disbelief and strangeness. She herself was feeling, and yet she was also seeing.

Then, she was Tony's, and the others, along with the noise of the water as it coursed past the side of the ship, became part of the symphony of life about which she had started to tell Tony.

Hers was so beautiful. Millie's was so awful. Rizzo was terrible. Tony was a god. Then for moments she didn't have any idea as to where they were. They could have been on a circus trapeze.

Noises from the deck brought her back. Millie was extricating herself. George was rolling over on his back. He grabbed the chair leg nearest him and began to pull himself up.

Millie, whose midriff was a mass of bunched-up clothing, was looking down at her breasts and at what she could see of her defoliated nethers. These parts were not in focus.

Taking ahold of George's shoulders, she was able to rise. An odd sight, with sagging stockings, variegated "life belt," bare hips, disclosed forest, and Andromeda's breasts.

She took stock of herself and began to make repairs. Up to this point, she had not been aware that others had been privy to the maneuvers.

Then she looked over at the back of Tony's head and Marian's eyes.

"Oops," she gasped. "Did you ever see anything like it?"

Marian smiled and felt the last of Tony.

"Let's go to the ladies' room," Millie suggested.

The thought came easily and seemed dictated by necessity.

"What the hell?" came from George.

"Not for you, Georgie," slurred Millie. "Just us girls."

By now, George was on his feet, swaying with the rhythm of the water's action and the now loud music from the ward room.

Tony, finally attracted by the light, turned around to gaze at the battlefield. He looked at the teetering shadow of George.

"Hello, George," seemed appropriate, and so he said it.

"Dark," replied George. "Didn't see you."

"I heard you," observed Tony, "but I thought you went up to the front."

"It was the front, all right," said George, letting out a coarse laugh. He was finding his second wind.

How Tony had gone through what he himself had experienced and had come out of it without a hair out of place should be a study in itself.

He patted George on the back, and the two of them went into the ward room. George went looking for a bathroom.

CHAPTER TWENTY SIX

Mr. Murphy and his young wife went to the master cabin to pass the night away in pursuits more interesting to Mr. Murphy than his conference with Clarissa Winship.

Midge was massaging her friend Harry's head. If this procedure was calculated to raise the dead, she was not being very effective.

Winship had retired to one of the smaller cabins.

"Shall I help you get Harry to bed?" Tony inquired of a worn-out Midge.

"Yeah, thanks. C'mon, Harry. Wake up. You're going to bed."

As this message passed through Harry's sense of understanding, he found it confusing. He did make an effort, though, and the three of them bumped and weaved into the passageway to the door of the cabin which was to be a safe haven for the worn-out Midge and a very shaky Harry.

The ship obviously had no cargo to deliver anywhere that night. The Captain sensibly secured it behind Angel Island and cut the engines.

Tony and Marian found their spot, as did Millie and Rizzo. They all fell asleep with little understanding of fellowship.

The next morning, the clever Captain had arranged sailor uniforms for all. The girls looked like they belonged in the cast of "South Pacific."

The ship sailed out the Golden Gate to Bolinas Bay, where it found an anchorage off the long sand spit near Stinson Beach. A picnic lunch was served on deck.

Rizzo, acting as if nothing had happened to him the night before, bobbed around like a tour guide. He was anxious for Mr. Murphy to understand the value of this Bay and these small coastal towns as way stations in the distribution system which was the backbone of their important business.

Mr. Murphy was anxious to indicate to Winship what he meant by way of "excitement" when President Parquez's ship came through. As they went back into San Francisco Bay, he showed her the spot at which he felt the sail-around would be effective.

"That'll take some doing with the Yacht Club," she explained.

"How many boats do you think you can drag out?"

"How does five hundred hit you?"

"Good; good. Great."

Winship knew that a hundred and fifty could create the scene needed.

Somehow or other, Tony, Marian, and Millie made their party clothing do for the debarkation. Rizzo, who had come onto the yacht early the day before, had a change of clothing. Tony drove Rizzo and Millie to Millie's Nob Hill place.

Marian and Tony dragged themselves back to the Bedford. They just had time to dress themselves so that Marian would look as if she had just made the bus ride from Santa Rosa.

When they arrived at the terminal, Marian crawled out of Tony's car with her "weekend" suitcase, blew Tony a kiss, and vanished into the station. She would wait until eight-thirty, when Harold and Mavis would come to pick her up. Twenty minutes late, Harold showed up. He had trouble getting his car started.

"You look sunburned," Harold observed.

"I tried not to," Marian countered.

"Well, you should have stayed out of the sun."

"It was nice, Harold. Restful."

The rest of the trip to the house was made in silence.

Mr. Murphy and his friend who, it turned out, was not his wife after all, took Harry and Midge back to their hotel. The following morning, they all flew back to Miami.

Clarissa Winship, by ship phone, had ordered a City car to meet her when the yacht landed.

She left with some minor problems. The one hundred and fifty grand she had picked up, she would share with her people. Rizzo's agent on the school run would come in for an extra share. He would probably ask for even more. Clarissa would have to be tough and tell him that he was in for more than the others already.

The Army contact, known as "General Letterman" was already skimming. Clarissa knew that. He wouldn't be difficult. Rizzo could also be handled.

The Mayor's cut would go neatly into his Widows and Orphans Fund.

His open-handed generosity was not a subject of any newspaper articles. However, a minor functionary in the Bureau of Internal Revenue had come across one of the transactions by way of a probate problem.

CHAPTER TWENTY SEVEN

There is, in San Francisco's great Federal behemoth, a small bureau whose main concern is fraud in tax exemption claims made by benevolent associations. This particular sub-agency was on a list to be merged with several other sub-agencies. It seemed that the tax collection from these sub-agencies was too small to sustain their bureaucratic effort.

Lowell Spisak, a square-jawed young lawyer type, who looked more like a high school basketball coach than a policeman, had received some last-gasp orders from the Bureau Chief to produce and produce fast, or else.

His first effort had been in trying to nail a tax exempt neighborhood organization whose stated purpose was to preserve the beach and shorefront environment. The suspicion was that the only environment involved was the beachfront of some wealthy people who did not share the Federal government's largesse and enthusiasm for providing recreational opportunities for four and a half million immediate members of the general public. Although "the people" were

represented in large numbers and with inflamma-
tory banners, the wealthy were represented by
five large law firms employing, in total, six hundred and fifty-seven lawyers.

The "people" lost that one, thus making
Lowell Spisak a threatened species himself. His
small domain was tottering. Just as he was about
to give up and go back to the family farm in
Iowa, he ran across the Widows and Orphans
Fund of Mayor Belpierre.

The Mayor's political connections were not
the political connections of the American President. An attack on this Mayor through bureaucratic channels promised a double payoff. Success
would knock off a political adversary and at the
same time prove the efficiency of the sub-agency.

All Spisak needed was to uncover one fake
entry . . . one payment where the beneficiary
was a nonperson. His section was desperate
enough to seize on such a straw.

It was a straw, and it was already waterlogged.

The list was before him. The beneficiaries
of the Mayor's Widows and Orphans Fund.
The first thing that caught his anxious eye
was the name of Emily Hanratty. The name
rang a bell.

He had, in the early days of his employment
in San Francisco, been cordial and finally intimate
with a hesitant young lady whose name was
Colleen Hanratty. He remembered trying to find

her once in the San Francisco telephone direc-
tory. He found her immediately. Very few
Hanratty's were listed. He mused for a moment
over his interlude with Colleen and vaguely wondered what had happened to her.

The next name on the list was O'Donnell,
Muriel. His bureaucratic sense of the practical
took him right back to Hanratty, Emily. He
sensed that there must be two hundred and fifty
O'Donnell's listed in the book.

He read the neatly clipped obit which accompanied Emily's name. Her husband, Fred, had
come from Olean, New York, where he had operated a successful cabinet shop. He had retired
and moved to San Francisco shortly afterwards.
His life in San Francisco was not spelled out in
detail.

Muriel's husband had come from Waco,
Texas, retired, moved to San Francisco. His
San Francisco experience did not reflect any
particular interest.

As Spisak checked backgrounds further, he was
impressed that when these presumed-deceased
persons arrived in the city, for the little the record
showed, they must have become senile, suffered
accidents which discouraged their activity, been
struck dumb, or contracted a social disease of
such virulence that reported societal contact was
at a minimum.

One thing for certain: they all left widows, and,

only occasionally, children. The children were generally located in some far-off place of little known name. Some orphans were left where parents had been killed in a common accident.

Such persons were Rosalie and Sydney. They were brother and sister, eight and eleven. Their name was Rebstock.

"Rebstock! Now there is an easy one," thought Lowell Spisak.

He abandoned Hanratty, Emily, and set in full pursuit of the Rebstock orphans. To his disappointment, he found them, now ten and thirteen, in the foster home of Mr. and Mrs. Milton Bask in the Sunset district.

Bask, before his retirement, had been a Division Supervisor of public school janitors. He was pictured with the Mayor in a prominently displayed photograph on the mantle in Bask's living room.

In all of his experiences he had never come across such grateful people as the Basks. Gratitude carried over into the joyful smiles of Rosalie and Sydney.

"That dear Mayor and his generous Fund," piped Mrs. Bask.

"Every month, just like clockwork," echoed her husband.

The house was neat and tidy and the children were well cared for.

Back to the drawing board dragged poor Spisak.

Clutching at straws, he was wondering vaguely if any of these widows had remarried. He spent some time looking through the marriage license records for Emily Hanratty to reappear. She did not.

He tried some other names. No luck. Finally, throwing caution and guilt for past negligence to the winds, he located Colleen Hanratty.

Colleen at first was surprised to hear from him, then gratified, then abrasive. Her memories of her last encounter with him, and its result, finally broke through her subconscious. The young and scared Lowell Spisak had not been a "gentleman." He had left her to her own devices. However, although seared memory there was, time had dimmed Colleen's homicidal intent. So, she agreed to see him.

He went to her place of work and waited for her. The least he could do was to take her to lunch. During the hamburgers and shakes, he told her of his new employment. She was impressed. He was coming up in the world. When she knew him, he had been studying law at night and working in the mailroom at the Bechtel Company during the day.

"What do you want, Lowell?" she queried defensively.

What she had received from him was probably

all she was going to receive from anyone. As his eyes narrowed, her face took on the look of a cornered mouse.

"I'm interested in the Hanratty family . . ." he started.

"About time." Her eyes did not relax.

He did not take up the point.

"I need to know about your Uncle Fred." He was playing a long shot.

"Uncle Fred?" Her tone indicated that she had no Uncle Fred.

"Yeah, the one who died three years ago."

"I don't have an Uncle Fred and I never did."

"You sure?"

"Listen, Lowell. I know my own family."

Lowell was crestfallen.

"What's the matter, Lowell? Don't you believe me?"

"I believe you. I was hoping you had an Aunt Emily."

"Lowell, that's very dumb."

"Yeah, I guess so." A pause . . . and then, a conditioned reflex. "Want to go to a movie tonight?"

Colleen became protective of whatever she had left. "Lowell, forget it," she replied.

"Okay, Colleen." He tipped the waitress and took the bill to the cash register at the door.

Colleen went back to her job, sorry that she had spoken so quickly.

The lonely Spisak returned to the Federal Building and went to his cubicle of power.

For a long time he looked at the name of Hanratty, Emily. It finally came to his mind that maybe Emily didn't exist.

Didn't exist!

Tax credits were being taken and payments made. She had to exist.

The Rebstock children existed. O'Donnell was past identifying. But Emily . . . a phantom pensioner?

Slowly in the mind of Lowell Spisak this fact, or nonfact, began to take form. Suppose none of these really existed? What then? He checked the phone book again with three other names pulled at random. None were listed.

He decided to check Laguna Honda Home in which San Francisco provides for its aged. Not one name appeared on his list. He checked death records for the last three years. Although the deceased husbands appeared, their presumed spouses did not.

Spisak was underpaid, but he was thorough. All public records were checked. The Rebstocks he found referred to several times. But not Hanratty, not O'Donnell, and none of the other three.

"Maybe they went back to Ireland," he thought. And then he checked the immigration lists. Emily Hanratty never showed. Then he decided to check Social Security. But if she existed at all, she had skirted through life without a Social Security number! Finally, Spisak closed the book. Emily was a nonperson. A nonperson!

Why was she on the list as a beneficiary of the City and County of San Francisco? Now, he was getting closer!

Someone was taking tax advantage for contributions paid out to a no one.

He took his file to his supervisor. His supervisor was a man of good memory.

"What happened to our rich friends and their tax exempt group? What about the environment of their front yards?" he queried. "What about the four million who need a beach?"

"It was decided that the public beach was good enough." Spisak paused. "But, here is a real funny one. It involves the Mayor's Widows and Orphans Fund. I have tried to trace a gal named Emily Hanratty."

"Who the hell is she?"

"She's on the Mayor's list of widows and orphans."

"She's an orphan? Poor kid."

"No kid, no orphan. She may not even be a widow. I think we should find out."

"Goddamn, the whole section is falling apart and we have to find a widow who isn't a widow!"

"Look, boss, I was pinning my hopes on those beachfronts."

"Well, it didn't work. What the hell is the

committee going to think when the Chief tells them that now we're pursuing nonexistent widows?"

"Someone is taking an exemption and making payments for people who don't exist."

"That went out with Tammany."

"This isn't vote fraud. This is Internal Revenue."

"How does the Fund get its money?" asked the supervisor.

Spisak, being inexperienced, had recognized the tree but not the forest. The basis for a great bureaucratic future.

"I'll look into that."

And so, the environs of the Mayor's grave site were identified for the first time. It wasn't in Colma. Yet . . .

CHAPTER TWENTY EIGHT

Leona had a busy weekend, without much help from Ralph. The children liked each other and played well together.

Mavis explained to Bubba that she had an 'Unca" who had built her slide in the backyard and brought her candy and coloring books.

"You don't have an 'Unca,' Bubba Too bad."

"I do, too." Bubba wasn't going to be left out.

"Yeah?"

"Yeah."

Bubba's little brother, Harvey, just looked back and forth as his elders discussed these matters. Somebody had given him candy, too! In his little head, he remembered that.

Just then, Leona came in to clean them up for lunch. Animal crackers and milk then became the principal concern for the youngsters.

CHAPTER TWENTY NINE

On Monday, Winship had a small meeting behind locked doors in her office. Although the people who attended wore epaulets of public authority, they had gathered to discuss some extracurricular business.

Winship went directly to the business of the day.

"Management likes the way you handle the schools," she said to Jack Clemens. Jack had heavy eyebrows and alert eyes.

"Glad to hear it; better to see it," he quipped.

"Greedy," said Winship, smiling as she gave him his envelope.

"As for you, McDivitt, your returns from the Presidio were a little low and your envelope reflects it. However, stay in there and you'll do O.K."

"Winship, you always do the right thing. I know that, or else I wouldn't be here," he said, pocketing the envelope without looking at it.

Clemens had carefully counted his. On finishing the job, he started to say something.

"Don't!" Winship beat him to the punch. He shut his mouth.

The meeting was over and Winship went off to see the Mayor. She had a contribution for the Widows and Orphans Fund to give him.

Mayor Belpierre, a prim little widower, was immediately available to Winship.

"Ah, Miss Winship. What a pleasure to see you."

"Mr. Mayor, you look very well," she oozed, looking down at him.

"Yes, yes. I try, I try. At my age, you have to keep moving. I do my best."

"Mr. Mayor," Winship zoomed in above him. "One of my old friends, a most generous man, has asked me to pass along a contribution, through you, to the Widows and Orphans Fund."

"Well, well. That's very kind," smiled Belpierre. "They do need help, and it's one of the happy things I do. Just to see this Fund grow and give happiness and added security to those poor folks. Yes, yes."

With this, Winship slipped the Mayor a heavy envelope.

"My word," the Mayor clucked as he felt the weight of the envelope. "Your friend has a heavy hand."

"He has indeed," laughed Winship.

"I hope our schedule will permit us to meet this generous person one of these days."

"Sooner than you think, Mr. Mayor."

"Oh?"

"Yes, he is a good friend of President Parquez."

"We are just planning for his visit," the Mayor beamed.

"That's right."

"Fine man, Parquez. His wife is coming, too. We'll have quite a time. He's very popular with our Filipino voters, my good friends."

"They're your friends, all right, and Parquez's visit won't hurt you at all. It will help you to hang on to the eleventh."

The eleventh was a voting district with a high Filipino registration.

"Mr. Mayor, I have an idea which I think will please you very much. My friend has a very large yacht. I think we can use it for the welcoming ceremony."

"Ah, a yacht. How will this work? Well, well, ah, we could have a regatta in his honor."

"You always have the great ideas, Mr. Mayor. You know he is arriving in one of his own cruise ships. We all could go to meet him at the Golden Gate. We could board his ship and welcome his party."

"Splendid, splendid. Will you please develop the plan?"

"If it's agreeable with you, let me involve the St. Francis Yacht Club and Treasure Island."

"Treasure Island, yes." The Mayor rolled around the word "treasure."

"I think I'd better get in touch with the Chief Protocol Officer in Sacramento, too. He is a jolly fellow and I'm sure he will be a great help in getting the State officers organized for the reception."

"Yes, yes. That's a good idea."

"Let me see what I can do and I'll report right back to you."

Winship again came close to the Mayor, who breathed deeply as he said goodbye.

She went back to her office, closed the door, and just sat there thinking.

CHAPTER THIRTY

While Winship had been in the Mayor's office, Tony went around to Marian's to find her tired and a little irritated. Her experience with Millie was just hitting her.

She was not her friendly, sweet self when Tony arrived.

"That goddamned Millie!" she attacked. "Some broad."

"C'mon, honey," winced Tony. "I still have a headache. My route was full of weekend junk and my truck acted up."

"I hope so." Marian really wanted Tony to pay for her fancied humiliation.

"Listen, baby, make me a fried-egg sandwich, O.K.?" Tony was pleading for peace.

Marian realized she was being a little hard on Tony. After all, Millie hadn't intruded too much on her turf.

"O.K., big Tony," she softened. "But I don't want that Millie anywhere near *you*."

"Don't worry, baby, don't worry."

Just then Mavis came in from the backyard.

"Hi, Unca Tony," she greeted. He tousled her hair. She laughed and ran to her mother.

"Bubba has an Unca, too."

Marian had not really picked up on what Mavis was saying, but Tony had.

"Let's give Mavis a jelly sandwich and juice for a snack. And then nappy-time. O.K., Mavis?"

"O.K., Unca," and then she pulled herself up on the chair.

Tony retreated to the living room, stretched out on the couch, and grabbed the paper. Mavis' snack eaten, she went off for her nap.

Marian curled up beside Tony and gave him a little kiss on the cheek.

"Tony, I have a real headache today. Really, I do. I just want to sleep."

"Let's."

And for the first time in their relationship, they really just *slept* with each other.

In the Philippine exile's office no one was sleeping.

CHAPTER THIRTY ONE

Not only Winship and the Mayor were concerning themselves with the Philippine President's arrival.

Juan Loredo was the exiled brother of the present Vice President. But for the perfidy of this Vice President brother, Juan would have been President of this insular friend of the United States.

Loredo and his partisan friends and their families had been forced to flee in the dead of night . . . the night the ballots were stolen and Parquez's great victory was announced to the world.

This had all happened several years before the currently-scheduled visit of Parquez to the United States.

Loredo and his friends had escaped to San Francisco where, with funds deposited long before, they started a bank. This was disheartening to the local bankers, since for some time local banks had been the custodians of the rebels' funds.

Having learned a lesson or two in American banking, these exiles made money hand-over-fist in their new venture Hence, the local disappointment.

The shipping firm in whose offices the meeting was being held was a front for other financial schemes being worked on by the rebels.

Today's meeting had been called by Juan's son and Miguel Caliente. They informed the others of the decoded telegram which advised of Parquez's planned arrival by ship.

The consensus of the meeting was that they should put on a "welcoming party" of their own. They would plan a reception that Francesco Parquez would remember for the rest of his life.

And, that "reception," if their plan succeeded, might indeed be "the rest of his life!"

Theirs wasn't the only headache planned for the Mayor

CHAPTER THIRTY TWO

Agent Spisak, intrigued by the "nonperson's benevolent society," went down to City Hall. After making inquiries, he found the person responsible for handling applications for the beneficiaries of the Fund. He put on a sad face.

"My name is Lowell Spisak," he informed the disinterested civic employee.

"So?" The employee was used to hearing people's names. Sounded the same, she thought. She only evinced interest when they got down to numbers. Those she understood.

"My aunt has just become a widow."

"Happens," the morose clerk responded.

"Her husband left her nothing, and there's no family but me. I'm on welfare."

On hearing "welfare," the employee perked up.

"How do I apply to get Fund assistance for my aunt?" Spisak asked.

"Take these papers and fill them out. You can do it over there." And the clerk shoved a sheaf of papers toward him.

It did not take Spisak long to realize that he

would need a Philadelphia lawyer to fill them out.

After a slight delay at a shaky table in a bad light, he approached the window again. The clerk was eating an apple and reading a paper She looked up.

"Yes?" she questioned.

"I don't think I can fill these out here. I don't know my aunt's Social Security number. And there are some other things I have to check on. Anyway, may I take these with me to fill out?"

"Sure."

And with that, Spisak was on his way back to his Federal perch.

CHAPTER THIRTY THREE

Several nights later, Tony and Marian shared a particularly agreeable time together. He was dressing and she was restoring the grotto to its normal drab appointments when the door downstairs opened and a light went on.

Harold had come home early!

Upstairs, lights went off. Marian hastily gave Tony a flashlight which she kept in the closet.

"Shine it in his eyes," she whispered urgently. Then she hissed "burglar" in his ear. Tony, normally not fast in emergency situations, was fast enough in this one. He grabbed the flashlight and headed for the stairs.

Harold's plodding feet approached.

Marian screamed, "Harold! Harold! Watch out!"

Tony yelled, "Out'a'my'way!" and shined the bright flashlight into Harold's face.

Harold's eyes contracted painfully. His conditioned reflexes jerked his hands into the air. One of them whacked Tony in the face as he went by

Marian was yelling bloody murder. Tony hit Harold in the stomach, forcing him to double up. Harold slipped down several steps. Tony pushed past him and out the door.

Marian shredded her old night dress and ran to a dazed Harold, who was now sitting on the steps rubbing his eyes and trying to catch his breath.

Marian shrieked, "Call the police, Harold! Call the police."

Harold was reeling. He staggered down the stairs to the kitchen, Marian behind him. Somehow they put the kitchen light on. They both grabbed the telephone. He, the receiver, and she, the dial.

At last they got the operator.

"We've been robbed," shouted Harold.

"Raped," corrected Marian.

"Huh? Oh, uh, get the police," yelled Harold into the phone.

Finally, in a garbled manner, their address was relayed to a Desk Sergeant. They had no sooner hung up the phone than they heard a siren. Not long after that, two big policemen came through the front door.

"I was sleeping," sobbed Marian.

"Yeah, I just got home. I was sick at my job," cried Harold

"Dear God!" sobbed Marian.

"Take it easy, lady."

"He was big," wheezed Harold, adjusting his glasses which had fallen off in the skirmish.

Marian's nightgown had been torn so that important parts of her upper chest were clearly visible to the investigators, who were trying to put to memory what they saw, before they put their eyes to paper to make notes. At first, no effort was made by Marian to cover herself. However, at the right moment, her point made, she gasped again and clutched her remnants about her.

Harold was pointing at the staircase.

Now, the San Francisco police force is made up of well-trained officers. Not only training but experience is the constant companion of these guardians of the night.

Each listened politely to the sobs and groans. Each took in the character of these victims of the storm. Each knew exactly what had happened. Each was surprised that more damage had not been done.

"Rape," gasped Marian.

"Hit me," gasped Harold.

"Yes, yes," regretted the Officers.

After many expostulations of sympathy, they promised the appearance of an Inspector the following day.

Next morning, Leona was horrified at Tony's black eye.

"You poor dear," she cooed, as she bathed it with cold water and put on a comfortable ice pack.

"Yeah," said Tony, "one of the cans fell off the truck."

Bubba was mightily impressed with the "shiner," as Tony jokingly referred to the discoloration. The child's inquisitive nature was not satisfied until his mother explained how shiners happened and how careful you have to be. Later, she heard him describing the phenomenon to his younger brother.

Since Tony didn't feel very well, he rested first in the living room and then, when the children were put down, he rested upstairs.

The condition of his eye did not affect his performance with Leona.

About two-thirty he arose and said his goodbyes.

He drove over to Marian's where Mavis was as concerned as Bubba over Unca's black eye.

Marian was concerned, too. She told Tony about the visit of the police. She said that a nice Inspector had arrived early that morning. He had told her how difficult it was to identify this type of intruder.

"They took a real report," she told Tony. "I said I'd been the victim of a rapist. I was crying and they believed me. The Inspector believed me, too."

"How about Harold?"

"He has a sore stomach. He didn't see anything. The second that flashlight hit his eyes, he was blind. He has something funny with his eyes. That's why he wears glasses."

"I'm glad to know that. It could come in handy later if you get raped again."

Marian smiled at him and said, "Anytime."

CHAPTER THIRTY FOUR

Winship called Rizzo. "The old guy is interested in the regatta."

"Great," responded Rizzo. "I've been thinking about that and how we're going to make the pick-up."

"From what they say, it will be pretty bulky."

"Yes, I'm sure," agreed George.

"Here's my idea. The boat we were on was a pretty good size. Can you get it again?"

"Of course."

"What do you think about putting the Mayor and his party aboard the cruise ship?"

"We can do that."

"Good. Then we'll go alongside the President's ship and put the Mayor and his party aboard so that they can ride with the President. I guess he will be able to get aboard all right. If he fell off the gangplank, it wouldn't be too much of a loss."

George Rizzo laughed at the idea.

"George, be serious," said a straight-faced Winship. "In the confusion of boarding, the materials will be delivered from the cruise ship to our yacht. It will look as if we're taking off presents from the President. How do you like that idea? And, while I have you on the line, what do you think about this? Maybe I can get Otto Luckner to spring luncheon for the 'royal' party on his riverboat?"

"Sounds good to me," said Rizzo. "Let's do it." He hung up and went back to the garbage business.

CHAPTER THIRTY FIVE

Several days later, Tony made a sizable delivery and picked up a large payment. He took this to Rizzo.

Rizzo called Winship and said he had a donation for the Widows and Orphans.

"Great!" exclaimed Winship. "Send it to my office with the donor's name."

"It will be over within the hour," Rizzo said and hung up.

Tony was standing there. Rizzo looked in the envelope, took several bills out for himself and gave Tony two bills.

"She wants me to send it over with the donor's name."

They tried to think of someone's name. Coming up with none, Tony suggested they might use Marian's. As Rizzo had a pile of work in front of him, he said O.K. "What's her name?" he asked.

"Marian," said Tony.

"I know that," snapped Rizzo. "What's her last name?"

"Oh . . . Fouts," Tony answered. Actually,

he never thought of Marian in terms of her husband's name.

"All right," grunted Rizzo, and he wrote in Marian Fouts. "You put in her address and, for God's sake, fill her in so that she'll know what to say if anyone asks her."

"Oh, sure."

"Poor old Thelma is down six times with all sorts of variations on her name. We'll give her a rest this time."

The envelope was delivered later in the afternoon to the Mayor, who beamed and hoped that his gratitude would be expressed to this generous contributor.

CHAPTER THIRTY SIX

On Saturday, Marian palmed off the "park detail" onto Harold. He would take Mavis to the merry-go-round. Marian packed them a picnic lunch and off they went. She also supplied Mavis with a bag of bread crusts.

First, they visited the swans at Stow Lake and then trekked to the merry-go-round. When the swans saw Mavis and her little bag of bread crusts, they all sailed in her direction and brought their friends.

"Look at that one, Daddy!" she cried as a large black swan pushed the others aside to get more than his share of the food.

"Very selfish," said Harold, eyeing two young lovers sauntering past.

After the crusts had been distributed to the excited swans, Harold suggested, "Let's go and ride the horses." The "horses" were on the merry-go-round. The sooner they were ridden, the sooner he could go home.

"Let's," agreed little Mavis.

On their way to the "horses," the cat (and it

was a big one) jumped out of the bag, figuratively speaking.

Mavis was trudging along when, all of a sudden, she looked up at her father and said, "Poor Unca Tony."

"Unca Tony?" questioned Harold in a matter-of-fact way.

"Yep. He has a shiner."

"He has a what?"

"A shiner."

"Uncle Tony has a shiner?" Harold was trying to understand, but not very hard.

"Yes, he does. Unca Tony has one."

Harold made an effort to make sense of what his daughter was saying. He thought she was playing some imaginary game.

"Uncle Tony," he repeated, as they walked along. He tried to make some connection with the Uncle Remus stories of his childhood.

"He told Mommie it didn't hurt."

Mommie? Tony? Oh, yeah. Thanksgiving. The moving-in guy. The fellow who had helped unload the truck.

"Yeah," thought Harold. "The big guy, Tony."

Then he turned to Mavis. "Oh, yeah, Mavis."

Harold was piecing it together. "Uncle Tony, big Uncle Tony, has a shiner?"

"Yes, big."

"Hmmm," wondered Harold.

"Unca Tony is good to me," Mavis was expanding. "He gave me a coloring book and crayons."

"And, candy?" Harold wanted all the facts.

Now, as has been said, Harold was not too quick, but he did see enough of the facts in front of him to be concerned about why some stranger to the family should give a little six-year-old girl a coloring book and candy and be called "Unca."

They went to the merry-go-round. Harold paid three times and was given one free ride. Mavis had chosen to ride a large and colorful tiger which went up and down and forwards and backwards as the merry-go-round circled melodiously. Harold held her on the beast, but his mind was elsewhere.

When they returned home, Mavis was bushed. Marian put her down for her nap. After childish protestations of gratitude and a short description to her mother of the black swan and the tiger, she fell fast asleep.

When Marian returned to the kitchen, Harold, like a jackal, was waiting for her.

"What's this about a shiner?" he pounced.

"A shiner?" His question meant nothing to her.

"Yeah, Uncle Tony's shiner."

She gasped imperceptibly. "Oh, that," she parried.

"Yes, that," hissed Harold.

"What about it?" Marian was at a loss.

"What's this business of Uncle Tony with the coloring books and the candy?"

Marian caught her breath.

"Oh, him. A can fell off the garbage truck and bopped him."

"What's he fiddling around Mavis for?"

"He's not 'fiddling around Mavis,'" Marian responded with some petulance. "She likes him. He put her slide up, which is more than you did."

"That was four months ago."

"It broke and he came back and fixed it."

"Well, I don't like him around our little girl. You gotta be careful."

"He's not 'around our little girl.' He came by a couple of times to say hello. He was sorry that he missed you."

"I'll bet."

"Now, look, Harold. If you're looking for a fight, just keep it up. I don't feel very happy about you coming home the other night all liquored up."

"For Chrissakes, all I had was some gin and gingerale with a couple of the guys after work."

"You were soused and you were brutal."

"For Godssake, Marian. I made a pass at my own wife. I have some rights, you know."

"Well, I wish you'd take them somewhere else."

"Tell that goddamned garbageman to stay away from Mavis."

"Oh, Harold. He's all right. He's a nice man. Mavis likes him."

"That's a fine thing to say. A six-year-old girl!"

And, the bickering went on, with Harold becoming more and more incensed by the minute, in the way of little men who fancy they have, at last, grounds for a loud and righteous complaint.

He railed on for thirty minutes more, and probably would have struck Marian, except that he held discretion the better part of valor. He had struck her once before, and she had laid him out! Once was enough, and this bout stopped short of physical violence.

CHAPTER THIRTY SEVEN

On Monday morning, Harold rose early and left the house in a surly mood. He went straight to the garbage company's office. He'd fix Mr. Tony, fiddling around with a six-year-old! Ha! Tony wouldn't keep his job long, once the garbage company management heard his complaint.

When he arrived, he asked the reception girl where he could make a complaint.

"Give it to me, Mister. I'll see that your service is corrected immediately."

"No, it's not that. I want to make a complaint about one of your drivers. I don't like his attentions to my six-year-old daughter."

The receptionist could see immediately that this was beyond the scope of her authority.

"I'll pass you along to Mr. Rizzo who is our General Manager."

After a moment on the telephone, she motioned Harold to the stairs that led to Rizzo's office.

Harold followed the directions and soon found himself face to face with Thelma in George Rizzo's outer office.

Thelma was impressed with Harold's serious appearance.

"Mr. Rizzo has gone out to the Yard, but he'll be back shortly."

"I'll wait," said Harold.

"What is your problem?" inquired Thelma in a kindly way.

"You got some guy here named Tony who works for you?"

"Yes, we do," Thelma warmed.

"He was fiddling around with my daughter," charged Harold the righteous.

Thelma cooled. "That's terrible."

"I'll say. Mavis is only six years old."

"Dear God in heaven! The monster!" Thelma gasped to herself.

"Oh, I've tried to be a good father. It's so hard. I work all night to keep my little family fed and then this happens."

"You poor man. Come sit over here," and she shepherded him with arms and hands to an old, leather covered chair

At her warm touch, a shiver went through Harold. Someone had been nice to him and he was responding.

He looked through his glasses at Thelma, who was backing away after having stashed him in the chair.

"Well, thanks," he murmured, and felt little stirrings.

"You've been hurt," she whispered quietly

"What's that?" He leaned forward.

"I said, you've been hurt and I feel for you. I know what it is to be hurt."

"You do? You have a six-year-old daughter, too?"

"No, but I know this monster."

She was going a little far. She was really thinking of Rizzo. She had noticed with Harold that her sympathy was hitting home and that he was beginning to take notice of her. She had stirrings, too.

Rizzo finally arrived.

To emphasize the importance of his complaint, Harold pulled out a small photograph of his family to better demonstrate the hearth which was being violated. Rizzo looked at it. He recognized Marian as someone he had seen someplace. He remembered the woman's name. Marian! He did not connect her with Harold. As Harold went through this outpouring of grief, Rizzo recalled the night of the yacht party. Then it suddenly dawned on him that Marian was Tony's girlfriend.

Carefully, he fully agreed with Harold and promised that steps would be taken against the man, who was obviously a fiend. He took Harold to the door of his office and asked Thelma to take care of him.

"Please get this man's telephone number at work and at home"

"I will, Mr. Rizzo," she promised and again

herded Harold to the big chair next to her desk.

Harold gave his telephone number at work, explaining again that he worked nights. He gave her his home phone number and then he did a surprising thing. On sort of a reflex, he asked Thelma for her phone number.

Before she realized what she had done, she had divulged this piece of personal information.

They said goodbye to each other, the bond of friendship forged.

CHAPTER THIRTY EIGHT

That afternoon, black-eyed Tony appeared on Marian's scene. Marian was quite upset when Tony told her of Harold's visit to the garbage company. She nearly collapsed.

Tony explained, "Your nut husband came to the office and raised hell! Made a complaint against me."

"Tony, what are we going to do? What did Rizzo say?"

"He didn't know who Harold's wife was at first, and then he damned near fell off his chair when he looked at a snapshot of your family which Harold gave him and he recognized you. Said I was bothering his six-year-old daughter."

"Harold said that!"

"That's what he said."

"You know, Tony, Harold's dumb and he's mean."

"Yeah, and he's also very upset. He wants me fired."

"We'd better be careful, Tony. I think you shouldn't come here until we can get a handle on this "

"Honey, I'll die."

"You may get yourself killed."

"Either way."

"I'll plan to come and see you."

"At the YMCA?"

"No, you find a place until this blows over."

"I'll try."

And so the poor lovers languished the rest of the afternoon.

The furniture in the master bedroom did not notice any problem.

CHAPTER THIRTY NINE

Downtown, in the caverns of the Federal Building, Lowell Spisak mulled over his facts. The Orphans had paid off. The Widows had not. There was one other group, and he recognized who they were.

"I guess I really should look at how this money gets into the Widows and Orphans Fund," he said to himself.

He went right back down to City Hall. This time, he went straight to the Mayor's Office. He explained carefully to the receptionist that he was working on a story about the Mayor's benevolences and would like to check the names of the Fund's donors since he would probably like to interview some of them.

He was taken downstairs to the office in which he had started to make an application for his "widowed aunt."

There he was introduced to an elderly bureaucrat who was obviously some old-timer's municipal secretary and girlfriend come upon a sinecure.

She was the guardian angel of the Fund.

"Ah, yes, the generous ones," she sighed. "You know, Mr. Spisak, it has always been a source of strength for me to know that out there in that cold, cold world there are generous people who are concerned about the problems of older women left as widows without adequate means of support."

"Isn't that the truth!" agreed Lowell.

"More than that, the orphans–the children left to destiny."

This old gal was a philosopher and damn near a poet, Lowell Spisak thought.

She brought forward a heavy ledger and, with a bookkeeper's alacrity, flipped open the pages.

Name after name.

"May I sit and go over this?" he inquired.

"Of course," she answered. "Please use this table."

Lowell did.

The entries were all made in the fine, round hand of someone who had learned to write before legible handwriting became a lost art.

Lowell spotted some well known names. Some were borne by libraries, zoos, and art museums around the town.

The latest entry was the modest sum of fifteen-thousand dollars. This amount had been generously provided by a Marian Fouts, whose address was given. Along with several others, Lowell marked it down. One of the other names was of a wealthy matron whom Spisak recognized

as the "Bongo Queen." Her father and grand-
father had made their fortunes in Bongo cereal.
She had taken these fortunes and quadrupled
them by clever investments.

He thought that a conference with her would
make an interesting interview. That is not exactly
what it turned out to be, since everything the
record reported was consistent with what the lady
said.

He then turned his attention to Marian Fouts.

In doing his prior investigations, he found that
a casual call without advance notice was the most
effective. His target, that way, had no time to
prepare answers.

He thought he would take Marian Fouts on
at four o'clock the following afternoon.

Finding where she lived was not difficult. He
climbed the front steps and rang the bell, then
stood to one side.

Marian answered the door and was obviously
surprised to see good-looking Mr. Spisak.

"Mrs. Fouts?" Spisak politely asked.

"Yes, I am," she responded.

"I would like to talk to you for a few minutes."

"I don't have much time," she said hastily,
looking over her shoulder as if to see the clock.

"This won't take long," Spisak assured her.

"Well, all right. Come in."

She took him into the living room and offered
the sofa. He sat down.

He quickly looked over the room and its

furnishings and concluded that the generosity behind the gift to the Widows and Orphans Fund had left very little for the general maintenance of this ménage. Being open-minded and imaginative, he began to ascribe this lady's generosity to a kindly heart dictated by some off-beat religion.

"Mrs. Fouts," he began, "I am visiting different donors to the City's Widows and Orphans Fund. I'd like to write an article on this subject. So far, the interviews have been very revealing."

"Uh, yes, Mr. Spivak."

"Spisak."

"Excuse me, Mr. Spisak. How can I help you?" Her mind raced to recall what Tony had told her.

"Well, you could tell me how you managed to save the money you donated to the Fund."

"Uh . . . my husband and I are . . . uh . . very frugal. He makes good money and . . . uh . . . our needs are not too fancy. We get along on very little. When we've saved up . . . uh . . . we look around for some . . . uh . . . charity . . ." Marian had a great imagination when stimulated. The story improved as it was told.

"You were impressed by the Widows and Orphans Fund, I take it?"

"Oh my, yes. We have heard of people who have been helped by the Fund. They must be very grateful to Mayor Belvoir."

"Belpierre?"

"Yes, Belpierre."

"Will you continue to donate to this Fund?"

"Uh . . . I guess so."

He asked a few more questions, some having to do with church affiliations.

Just as he seemed satisfied with the answers to his questions, Tony bounced in, after opening the front door with his key.

"Hi, baby, I'm here," he yelled, not seeing Marian and her guest. "Oh, I'm sorry. I didn't see you. Hi, Marian."

"Oh, Tony. This is Mr. Spirak, excuse me, Spisak. He is making a study of that Fund."

"A study, huh? What'cha doing that for, Spisak?"

"We want to put together a basis for awarding the Mayor a medal. What Mrs. Fouts tells me is very helpful. What do you know about the Fund, Mr. uh . . . ?"

"Name's Tony. Well, I know that a lot of widows and orphans are being taken care of."

"Yes, I thought it might be interesting to interview some of the generous donors," said Spisak.

"That's Marian," Tony replied off-handedly.

"Yes, many of the donors are very rich people. I can't help but notice that you and Mrs. Fouts must have to forego many nice things to afford such gifts."

"Well, I'm not . . . uh . . . why, yes we do. I make good money. We don't need a lot." Tony was a little edgy.

Mavis ran through the room. "Unca Tony, you don't have your shiner any more."

Tony looked at the child and then returned to Mr. Spisak.

"Mrs. Fouts' child from another marriage."

Marian nodded and, for some reason, her subconscious began to compare these two men. During the next few minutes, the conversation was very general.

At last, Mr. Spisak rose to leave. He gave one long look at Marian and hoped he would have occasion to see her again. Mavis had snuggled next to her.

"Well, I want to thank you very much. May I call you if I need any more information?"

"Of course you can." And, she gave him her telephone number.

Tony took him to the door. When he returned, he was not smiling.

"How long was that guy here before I came in?"

"Not very long," answered Marian.

"What'd'ya tell him?"

"Not very much. He seemed to think we gave this money because we're generous. He asked what religion we belonged to. I told him we were Catholic."

"Anything else?" Tony was not nice-Tony now; he sounded like tough-Tony.

"No." She paused. "Tony, honey, why were we so generous?" she queried.

"The Mayor likes it that way. So does Rizzo."

"Rizzo! Does he have something to do with this?"

"Baby, don't ask a bunch of questions."

"Now, look here, Tony. You used my name. I think I should know what the game is."

"Take it easy, baby."

"No, Tony. I want to know."

"Don't push, baby. It's not nice."

"What do you mean, 'not nice?'"

"I mean it could be uncomfortable to ask questions. Rizzo doesn't like that."

"The hell you say."

"The hell I say. And, the hell with it." He tried to change the subject. He made a move to kiss her. She backed away.

"Hey, baby, what's this?"

"Look, Tony. You have used my name and that bozo was looking for something. I don't want to get mixed up in it."

"You are mixed up in it, baby."

"Tony!"

"Yes, you sure are, and, so am I."

"You may be, but I'm not, and I'm not going to be. There's something phony about those friends of yours . . . Mr. Murphy, Harry.

A couple of slobs, and that Rizzo is a creep!"

"Now, baby . . ." started Tony.

"Don't you 'baby' me. You get out of that mess. I don't want to be any part of it."

"Nuts! Marian. I'll see you tomorrow . . . maybe."

"Get out of it, Tony. I mean it."

"Drop it, Marian."

"I will not."

He slammed out of the house.

She began to cry.

This upset for Marian was nothing compared to the dumping of misery that was to beset Leona.

CHAPTER FORTY

Tragedy struck suddenly, just before noon, at the Holiday Sureway.

Fat Ralph turned to speak to one of his co-workers, and he short-circuited the heavy electric cutting instrument that he was holding. He backed into some spilled water. That did it. Ralph lasted about four seconds. He was electrocuted. He fell against the butcher block which had been his friend. He was still shaking.

Someone pulled the main switch. Ralph and his knife fell to the floor.

The electric connection was disengaged. Ralph was rolled onto his back. Somebody tried to administer artificial respiration but it was obvious that Ralph was no longer an employee, or a husband.

There was a great deal of running around. An ambulance came and carried off Ralph's mortal remains.

The Store Manager jumped into his car and drove to Ralph's home. He rang the bell and waited. Then he rang it again. After some time,

Leona answered the door, flushed, and in her robe.

The Manager was a little surprised that, in the middle of the day, she was practically unclothed.

"Oh, Mr. Fineman!" Leona squeaked when she finally got the door open. "What a surprise!"

Not seeing a smile on Fineman's face, she gasped, "There's been an accident!"

"Yes, Mrs. Remmer, an accident."

"Oh, God."

"Ralph has been seriously hurt."

"Oh, God."

Tony bounced down the stairs. "What's the commotion?" he inquired.

Fineman, already confused by Ralph's demise, was not prepared for what he saw to be the fact.

Poor Leona collapsed into Tony's arms. Then, between the two of them, they helped her to the sofa. She was shaking and sobbing.

"What the hell has happened?" demanded Tony.

"Mr. Remmer electrocuted himself at the store just now."

Fineman thought that Leona was out of it; she wasn't.

"What do you mean?" she cried. "Ralph . . . what's wrong with him? Is he dead?"

"Mrs. Remmer, he never knew what hit him."

Normally, that piece of information is supposed to bring solace to the bereaved.

Leona let out one long wail and grabbed Tony. Tony could hardly breathe, her hold was so tight.

"Oh, Tony, Tony, Tony!" she sobbed.

Fineman was beginning to get the picture.

"He was a fine man, Mrs. Remmer, a fine man."

"Thank you, Mr. Fineman," she said over her shoulder, with effort. "He was my husband. Not a bad man . . . not a good one. He was a bully," and let out another wail.

It is odd how, in one moment, when seized by deepest grief, some manage to find relief in two or three succinct words of derogatory truth. Leona tried to get control of herself and did.

"Oh, Mr. Fineman, thank you for coming here yourself."

She straightened herself out, arose from the sofa, and smiled at him.

He was without words.

Tears only made her more beautiful. Tony stood near her.

Fineman finally became aware of the incongruity of this beautiful widow of the last hour standing heroically next to this tall, bronzed man with a large green and yellow bath towel pulled around his middle.

He smiled in response to the smile he received from Leona Remmer.

She came over to him and said quietly, "Please excuse what you see, Mr. Fineman. It's all the love I have."

Fineman's eyes filled.

"I understand, Mrs. Remmer, I understand. I'll help you . . . I will. Anything." His fluency and store manager-front fled completely in retreat.

Bubba, followed by Harvey, came down the stairs and into the living room, dragging their blankets with them. Leona bent forward and clasped them to her.

"Daddy won't be home for supper," she said. And that was that.

"Goodie! We can watch t.v.!" Bubba was happy.

CHAPTER FORTY ONE

As if the shock of Ralph's accident wasn't enough, Leona went through one more traumatic experience which should have completely shattered her.

Later, after Tony left, Leona called Marian to tell her what had happened. She came right over, bringing Mavis.

When she arrived, she found Leona in control.

"God, what a terrible thing, Leona!" she cried, as she took her sister in her arms.

"At least it wasn't the children," Leona quieted her sister.

Then they were speaking of various things which would have to be done and the kids were playing in the living room

Mavis was looking at Bubba saying seriously, "Unca Tony had a terrible shiner. That's a black-eye, Bubba. It's all better now."

"My Unca had a shiner, too."

"My Unca's shiner was bigger than your Unca's!" the kids were yelling at each other.

Marian came in. "Now, now. Be quiet. It's

not nice to yell like that. Poor Uncle Ralph hurt himself."

"He's not coming home for dinner," Bubba announced.

"Bubba says his Uncle had a bigger shiner than Unca Tony," Mavis yelled.

Marian thought they were talking about Ralph. Leona heard Mavis say, "Unca Tony."

"What did you say, Mavis?" she asked above the hub-bub.

"I said Unca Tony had a bigger shiner than Bubba's Unca ."

Leona started to ask, "Bubba's Uncle? Who's that?"

Then, it slowly dawned on her that both "Uncas" were one person named Tony. How could that be?

Marian was not so quick.

"My Unca had the biggest shiner," Bubba yelled through the noise.

By this time, both mothers started herding the children into the backyard to play.

Leona returned to the house and when Marian came into the kitchen, she asked, "Marian, what in the world does all that mean?"

Marian started, "Well, I have a boyfriend. You know him. Mavis calls him Unca Tony."

Leona sat down. "Tony?"

Marian said, "Yes. Tony. You remember the fellow who helped me move in. He's been fun.

Lots of fun, but I think the s.o.b.'s mixed up in the rackets."

"Tony? Your boyfriend? Marian, that's terrible!"

"No. It's been great. But, I think it's over now. He walked out yesterday."

"Walked out?"

"Yeah, we had a big fight. I don't like his goon friends. They had my name on something, and the nicest guy from the government came to talk to me about it. He's coming back tomorrow to see me again. Well, that is, tomorrow, if he doesn't interrupt anything you need me for."

"Marian, you've been having fun with Tony?"

"Yeah, fun."

"So have I."

"So have you what?" asked Marian, not understanding the drift of the conversation.

Leona looked straight at her. "I've been having 'fun' with Tony, too."

The lights suddenly went on in Marian's head.

"You, too, huh?"

"Me, too."

"The son-of-a-bitch!"

"No, not the son-of-a-bitch."

"The bastard!" Marian yelled. "He never even told me."

"Marian, really, how dumb do you think he'd have to be to tell you a thing like that?"

"Dumb," croaked Marian. "And me putting out and I never even suspected."

"You dumped him, Marian?"

"You can say that again."

"Well, I love him."

"I thought I did."

"I do." Leona was firm and sure.

"Lee, baby. What a terrible thing to have happen, and right on top of the other."

"No, Marian. It's not terrible. It's hard to believe, but it's not terrible."

"Well, I don't want him. Anyone who'd do a thing like that. And me, pushing Harold around."

"Don't even think of it, Marian. Find somebody else. Just leave Tony to me. I'll straighten him out."

"You can have him!"

"Thank you, little sister."

CHAPTER FORTY TWO

The next few days were hectic. The children had to sort out the fact that they all had the same "Unca Tony," and, in the way little children have of accommodating themselves, Mavis and Bubba made their peace. Harvey didn't even know there had been an argument because his Unca Tony was still there.

Mr. Spisak came by the following afternoon. Marian fixed some cake and coffee for him.

"You know, Mrs. Fouts, I'd sure like to speak to your husband."

"He's at U.P.S. Does shipping. Works nights." Marian glossed over the unimportance of her husband's work. She was concentrating on the bird in the hand.

With eyes cast down, she related to him the sad facts of Ralph's fatal accident.

She hesitated in just the right places. Lowell was afraid he was invading the privacy of the bereaved. He tried to be business-like. However, before he left, young Spisak had been conquered. He took Marian by the arm and looked deep into her eyes, while commiserating with her over the loss of her brother- in-law. He sent his condolences to her sister.

"I'll tell you something, Lowell," she confided, getting very near to his face and nose which was devouring the lilac perfume. "My sister isn't going to miss him for five seconds. She's in love with a big hunk of a man who delivers." She nearly said, "From door to door."

If there had not been a death in the family, Lowell Spisak would have kissed her. Marian, not used to such reserve, was disappointed.

Lowell returned to his Federal hutch in the sky. The place had an aura of beauty.

He wondered about Marian's husband. He'd pay him a visit as soon as possible at his office. He'd just call there unannounced. Mr. Fouts worked nights, he'd been told by Marian. Have to handle him carefully. He was big and impressive. For a man who worked nights, he had quite a tan.

CHAPTER FORTY THREE

The arrival date for President Parquez was set at last. Winship was informed by the Mayor's secretary. She and Winship had a thing going, and the information was passed along over lunch at Modesto Lanzone's.

"Good. Thanks a lot, dear," said Winship. "We'll have to pull our final plans together now."

"How many will that yacht hold? The Mayor will probably have six thousand requests."

"Some people will have to be disappointed," rejoined Winship with a laugh.

"Seriously, though, how many?" the secretary asked.

"Rizzo told me thirty would be a good number."

"Rizzo? Is he mixed up in this?"

"It's his boat."

"Just wanted to know. I have to put that damn list together."

"You have a pleasant chore."

"Guess we'll have to use the number-seven list."

"The number-seven list?"

"Yes, we have twenty-two lists," the secretary divulged. "Number twenty-one is an open reception at City Hall. Everyone. With no drinks and no food."

"I should think so. What's number seven?" queried Winship.

"That is when the Mayor has some ethnic group invited. We'll pull the Philippine list and chop it. Include just the community leaders and club presidents."

"Rizzo should be on the list."

"God, he's a creep. But, it is his boat."

"I think you'd better figure a party of four for Rizzo. We should know exactly how many will be expected because Otto Luckner is going to give a 'riverboat luncheon' in their honor."

And then some other notes were made. "You'll go, too, won't you?"

"Wouldn't miss it for the world."

"Well, that's that. See you tonight."

"Sure. I'll have the tickets."

"Great."

They walked back to City Hall together.

CHAPTER FORTY FOUR

Rizzo had not forgotten Millie after the famous boat trip. He had spent an unforgettable night with her in her small Russian Hill apartment. He spent the other nights there as well, telling his wife that he was in Sacramento or some other place.

As Rizzo's infatuation with Millie grew in intensity, he suggested that he help her to find a bigger place. They spent several weekends looking and at last they found a neat hideaway on Telegraph Hill. Rizzo loved the place. From the porch outside the living room window, he could see the Bay. In the window itself, Coit Tower was framed. It loomed like a great phallic invitation. He bought the condo and a garage. She made him put it in both of their names.

Millie worked in the public relations office of one of the leading hotels. As such, she was able to invite Rizzo to business-sponsored parties for which the hotel was responsible. The two of them were something to see. At one of the parties, who should they run into but Clarissa Winship!

"Rizzo, I want to thank you for helping to

set up the yacht for the Parquez visit," Winship conveyed in a quiet moment.

"Always want to help, Clarissa. You know that," he responded.

"Want to bring Millie?"

"Thanks for asking. She'll love it, won't you, Millie?"

Millie, with memories of the last boat ride, readily agreed.

"Great," said Winship.

"You got it," Rizzo agreed.

CHAPTER FORTY FIVE

After his dinner, Lowell Spisak decided to call around at the U.P.S. warehouse. When he arrived there shortly after seven, he showed the guard his identification badge and said he'd like to interview Mr. Fouts. The guard called the section supervisor and Lowell was directed to an office near a large sorting area.

He waited for about ten minutes. Then the door opened and, to his surprise, a short, thin, sandy-haired fellow with glasses stood before him.

"I'm Harold Fouts," the little fellow said in a faltering voice. Harold thought he was being called on the carpet for something he had not done or for something he had done wrong.

Spisak, used to surprises, didn't miss a beat. "Oh, ah, Mr. Fouts. Your wife is Marian Fouts?"

"Yes, she is, but she doesn't have anything to do with this place."

"What do you do here, Mr. Fouts?"

"I am a sorter in the small box and envelope department."

"Been here long?"

"About six and a half months."

"Like your work?"

Harold thought, "They're going to fire me."

"Yeah, I like it. I like working nights. I have trouble with my eyes in bright daylight."

"Is that so?"

"Yes."

"Do you have any children, Mr. Fouts?"

"Yes, I do. Mavis. She's six." As an after-thought, Harold asked, "Are you from the garbage company?"

"I'm from . . ."

"That goddamned Tony!" Harold inter-rupted. "He ought to get it. Fiddling around with my daughter."

"Oh?"

"Mr. Rusto must have sent you."

"We're just checking some information. Ever hear of the Widows and Orphans Fund?"

"The whose?"

"The Widows and Orphans Fund."

"What's that got to do with Tony?"

"I don't know."

"Never heard of it."

"I want to thank you, Mr. Fouts."

"Oh, that's all right. That s.o.b. should be behind bars. A six-year-old child yet!"

"We're looking into it," said the bewildered Spisak.

They shook hands and Lowell left, still trying to equate Tony and Harold.

He went home and was preparing for bed when Harold's question came home loud and clear . . . "What's Tony got to do with the Widows and Orphans Fund?"

Lowell interpolated the question to pick up the fine points which he had missed before. And, who was Mr. Rusto?

"What's Tony got to do with it?" Good question.

While he was passing himself off as Marian's husband, Tony certainly sounded as if he knew about the Fund. He must have known about the facts which Marian related to him. Where else could she have picked up such information?

"Yes," said Lowell Spisak to himself. "I'm going to keep that guy in sight."

And he went to sleep as if he had accomplished something.

CHAPTER FORTY SIX

When Spisak left him, Harold went back to the sorting room. Spisak had scared him. Harold wondered why the garbage company was sending a guy like that to see him. He thought that they should be after "that goddamned Tony." Widows and children . . . what the hell was that all about? Must be something to do with Mavis. Rusto, he'd know. He thought again. The mention of Rusto reminded him of Thelma. She was nice to him, he reminisced. "I'd like to see her again," he thought.

He sorted a couple of pieces of material in front of him and looked up at the wall clock. He noticed that it was only eight-fifteen.

"Geez! It's not too late." And he started through his pockets to find her phone number.

Between the sorting table and the employees' pay phone, he decided he'd go over and see her tonight, if she'd let him.

He looked at the number on the paper, clunked money into the slot, and dialed.

The phone rang.

The flat voice of Thelma answered.

"Hello, Thelma. This is Harold Fouts," Harold announced.

"I beg your pardon? What did you say?" came uncertainly from Thelma.

"I'm Harold. Harold Fouts," he repeated.

"Oh, hello Mr. Fouts. This is a pleasant surprise." The voice became warmer.

"Thelma, I'd like to come and see you." Who would have thought that Harold had it in him!

"I'd like to see you, too, Harold."

"How about right now?"

"Well . . ." Thelma made it last a long time. "I was going to bed."

"I won't stay long," Harold promised.

"All right. But, not long, Harold. I have a hard day tomorrow."

"I'll come right over. What's your address?"

She gave him an address on Noriega just off 19th Avenue. He jotted it down next to her phone number.

Harold went to the men's room, washed his hands and face, and patted his hair. He put on his coat.

He then went to the supervisor's office. He explained that he did not feel well and would head for home. He was willing to take on a Saturday detail to make up. The supervisor made a mark on his record.

Harold left the building and found his old car. For once he did not have to coax and plead. It started right up and off he went.

Once on 19th Avenue, he drove toward No-riega. He made the proper turns and found Thelma's house. It had belonged to her father and mother. She had lived in it most of her life. When he came up the front steps, she was at the door with the hall light behind her.

"Come in, Mr. Fouts," she invited.

He did.

"Please call me Harold," he mumbled.

She closed and locked the door.

"Can't be too careful," she smiled.

He felt secure.

"I made some chocolate and some old-fashioned cookies."

"Just like my mother used to do." Harold was charmed.

"You come right in here, Harold. Take your jacket off if you like. My Dad always used to do that. That's his comfy chair. Please make yourself comfortable."

What a new experience for Harold. Someone was being nice to him.

Although his eyes were grateful for the dim light, it took them some time to accommodate the frugal lighting system. Maybe the lights were low because Thelma thought it might be more friendly to her face.

Thelma was "thirty nine." She was not faded, but the process had started. She, of course, thought it had proceeded farther than it had. There were still traces of Thelma's youth to be seen. She had stayed close to home, first helping her mother to take care of her father and then nursing the mother. Now she shared the care of an old aunt, who lived with one of her married sisters.

Sex to Thelma was a necessary adjunct to her job. She, of course, had heard of the penalties exacted against employers stemming from the sexual harassment cases. She had also heard of women who had been fired or not rehired because they stood up for their rights.

In these matters she was timid. Besides, what harassment she underwent to keep her job at the garbage company wasn't all that painful to her.

Sometimes she went to work in the morning resolved that she was going to stand up to Mr. Rizzo. But, resolution faded as the day wore on. She had started with the hope that something would come from her relationship with Rizzo. Sort of a last glimmer of hope.

She had always liked Tony, but he only kidded her. That one night when he came over to sit with her aunt had been a fiasco. The old lady, thoroughly rested from sleeping through most the day, was energetically wide-awake during his whole stay. She refused to go to bed. She kept interrupting. If they went out into the kitchen together, the old lady would yell for something. Finally, they had to give up any thought of intimacy.

Both of Thelma's parents were now dead and she had this house to herself, just like apparently she had herself to herself.

The house had been paid for long since. Now, Harold's visit was an event in a life devoid of events. She had spruced herself up. Harold had to say to himself that what he could see of her was attractive.

She had another asset. She could play the piano. It was a studied and measured talent, not the type of talent which makes one the life of the party.

Harold spied her upright piano in the dining room.

"You play the piano, Thelma?" he asked.

"Yes, I do. I'm not great, but I can make do."

"My mother played the piano," Harold reminisced.

"Would you like to hear my new piece, Harold?"

"Oh, yes, I would." And he moved toward the dining room.

Thelma took her cue and settled herself before the antiquated instrument. She cleared her throat as if she were about to sing.

This threw Harold off for a moment. Then she struck a chord and he came back on track.

She proceeded to play a pedestrian piece of music without much variety or expression. She seemed to get all the notes right.

Harold was entranced. However, he did not keep time with his foot.

When she completed the recital, she suggested they have the chocolate which was warming in the kitchen.

"I always have a cup of cocoa before I go to bed," Thelma confessed innocently.

Harold's heart leapt. Then Thelma realized the suggestiveness of her remark. In her confusion, she bustled through the kitchen door, the strong spring of which brought the door back unexpectedly into Harold's face. There was a dull thud and his glasses were knocked to the floor.

"Oh, my goodness!" cried Thelma. "I've hurt you!"

"I'm all right. Nothing at all."

He tried to make her feel better. His nose was sore and he rubbed it.

"Are you really all right?" she breathed anxiously.

"Yes, yes. All right." And he felt around on the floor for his glasses. Finding them, he put them back on his nose and carefully went into the kitchen.

It was a nicely curtained area with a cheery table in an alcove. Thelma had set up a hastily prepared little feast for this homey moment.

"Sit down, Harold, and I'll get the cocoa." And she turned to the stove where it was warming.

Harold was hungry. He slipped a raspberry jam covered cookie into his mouth. Thelma saw him. He looked just like a bad little boy caught with his hand in the cookie jar.

"Go ahead, Harold. Help yourself," she laughed, and, at that moment, he saw a younger, prettier Thelma than he had anticipated.

She poured the chocolate into the china pot which she had also warmed and brought it to the table.

"Here you are, little boy. To go with the cookies." She was being motherly and coy at the same moment.

Harold loved it. The chocolate was finished to the last drop and only one cookie remained.

"Put it in your pocket, Harold, for future reference. Here, I'll put it in a paper napkin for you."

Harold was transfixed. He didn't want to go home. He looked around the comfortable kitchen. His mother's kitchen in Oklahoma had been like this one.

With a warm smile at Harold, Thelma placed the soiled china on the sink without a sound. Marian always did this with a bang loud enough to crack it.

"You must come again, Harold."

"I will, Thelma. I will. Maybe Saturday, if you're going to be here."

"I'll be here, Harold. Just try to call in the morning and let me know what time."

They went through the small home to the front door.

"Thelma, I loved this evening. Thank you so much."

"It has meant a lot to me, too, Harold."

He put his hand out to shake hers. She did the same. They could have been on the public square any place.

"I'll come over Saturday."

"I'll be waiting."

And then she opened the door. Harold went outside, down the steps, around to his car, and waved goodbye to her. She waved back. He climbed in behind the steering wheel.

He put in the key and depressed the starter. No response. He did it again. No response. He waved to Thelma. She waved back. The third time, the car choked twice and finally caught.

He sped away from the curb, fearful that if he tried to wave to Thelma again the car would stop dead.

The last she saw of him was the tail light of the car which was flickering uncertainly.

Thelma turned and went back into her house, closed the door and leaned against it, like they do in the movies. She was warm inside.

For the first time since she had been very young, she was truly happy. She had found a friend.

CHAPTER FORTY SEVEN

Harold had experienced something during Thelma's piano recital. He became excited and guilty at the same time. The excitement made him think. Before the dulcet notes of Thelma, excitement had been ripped out of him by a frantic Marian.

As he drove his dilapidated car home, he began to compare. Sweet music. Clinging, grasping, cloying hands, arms, legs, lips, the frantic efforts of a miner when the promised vein runs out.

Only, the vein hadn't run out. The beautiful pedestrian melody of Thelma had proven that to him.

He was missing something in his life. What he had once been afraid of, no longer was fearful to him.

But, he was honest. Real honest. And, he was pursued during these moments of reflection by guilt.

Somehow, he had to take the bull by the horns. The thought began to excite him again. He found his house. The house of Marian and Mavis. Not wishing to be clobbered again, he went up the front steps with some concern for his future well-being.

He opened his door, looked inside, and flicked on the light. Again, he peered around. Then he went upstairs.

Marian was in bed. He went into the bathroom, gargled, and left his clothes. He pulled his striped pajamas from a hook, and, after turning the light off, went into the bedroom. Marian had rolled over.

Surprise of surprises, she had rolled over in his direction. He crawled under the connubial covers. He was seized by urgent hands.

"No, Marian. No!" he gasped, before she could proceed further.

"What?" she said in her sleep. "Ton . Harold? What the hell? Oh, come on, Harold. I need."

Harold was resolved. "So, what else is new?"

Not very polite. However, it did get him started and not to exercise any of his connubial rights.

"Oh, come on, Harold!" And she reached for him. He jackknifed and rolled away from her. Whatever he had, diminished in fear.

"Marian," he said, matter-of-factly, "we've got to talk."

"Harold, it must be two o'clock."

"Maybe, it is, but we gotta talk."

"Harold, give it to me and go to sleep."

"No, Marian. I'm not going to give it to you now, or, ever again."

Marian couldn't believe what she was hearing.

"Ever again?" she repeated.

"Ever again," he said from his side.

"Now, Harold . . ." She thought it was a joke, or maybe Harold had been reading some sex book which advised holding off until both parties were crazed by desire.

"No more 'now, Harold,'" he said in a calm and unexcited voice.

She staggered out of the bed on her side and turned on the light to see if this was the right Harold.

It was.

"Now, what the hell is this?" she repeated.

"I have something to tell you, Marian."

"You have something to tell me?"

"Yes, I do." He was sitting up now in the light Marian had managed to turn on.

Marian was slightly disheveled, but beautiful through it all. Ninety-nine men out of one hundred would have seized her where she stood, silhouetted against the otherwise unkind light. Harold was number one hundred. He did not seize her. He put on his glasses. He still didn't seize her.

"Marian, I'm leaving."

"You're what!"

"I'm leaving you "

"That's a fine thing to say after all I've done for you . . . just 'I'm leaving.' A fine, god-damned thing."

"Well, I am."

"What about Mavis?"

"She'll get along all right, and so will you."

"What do you mean by that crack?"

"Marian, look at you. Five minutes after I'm out of the house, you'll find somebody."

"Harold!"

"Come off it, Marian. You know you'll get along."

"Well, I'll be godamned."

"It's not that bad, Marian."

"Your laundry, Harold, your dinner . . . ?"

"I'll manage somehow, Marian."

"Harold?"

"Yeah?"

"You gotta girl?"

"Now that you ask, Marian, I think I have."

Marian sat down on the side of the bed and just laughed. She could not control herself. All she could gasp—when she could pull herself together—was, "Well, good luck. Good luck, Harold."

"Thanks, Marian," he smiled as he crawled back into bed. "I was hoping you'd understand."

CHAPTER FORTY EIGHT

Late the following afternoon, Rizzo and Winship met at the Marin boathouse. He was always a little uncomfortable with Winship. She was attractive, certainly, but there was a mannish quality that Rizzo recognized. This warned him to keep his hands off. Besides, she was four inches taller.

Winship walked in with the firm stride of a prize-fighter and went right to the point.

"We've got the marching orders. We're organizing the flotilla."

She asked for a beer. Rizzo rummaged in the refrigerator and found one. They both sat down, enjoying the reflections of a beautiful sunset on the Bay.

"Say, Rizzo, by the way, schoolyard sales are down."

"Clemens told me the cops are around," responded Rizzo.

Winship was surprised. "I thought we had it fixed."

"New cops, I guess."

"Well, anyway, private school sales are doing

great." Winship was pleased to pass on this information.

"Clemens told me. He's bright. They put the heat on one place, he goes across the street."

He paused and then added, "Well, what is your plan?"

"I'm going to have a little talk with one of the Commissioners," she said.

"Not that. I mean the Philippine job."

"The Mayor's secretary and I have made up a guest list. You'll have four places."

"I think I'll ask Mr. Murphy. He wants to come out."

"Tell him not to bring that Harry. He's a lost cause. He has only to look at a cork and he gets drunk."

"Mr. Murphy likes him."

"Try not to have him. The Mayor won't like him." Winship was firm.

Rizzo changed gears.

"I have been trying to work out how to handle the President's party and I think it would be better if we have them come aboard the yacht, rather than us going on to the cruise ship."

Winship agreed. The yacht could make a quick circle of the Bay, which a cruise ship could not. The Mayor wanted to show the President the freight facilities which were being developed.

Rizzo felt that the payment for the cases could be handled on the yacht. He'd have control of the goods.

"Payoff and delivery. Nice and clean. Then we'll deliver the party to Pier 9 for their fancy lunch. As soon as that's done, we can take the yacht over to the old marina and have a little party of our own with our customers."

"Rizzo, that's good thinking. Where will we pick up this tribe?"

"I think right off the St. Francis Yacht Club."

"The whole world will be there."

"Yep. All watching the President and the Mayor. If we try to make contact before they reach the Golden Gate Bridge, somebody might notice. But, with the guns going off at the Presidio, the boats circulating, and all that other activity, I don't think anyone will notice."

"Rizzo, you're a steel trap." Winship snuffed out her cigarette.

Rizzo took this for a compliment.

CHAPTER FORTY NINE

During his luncheon, Lowell could not get Tony and "Rusto" out of his mind.

He thought perhaps Marian would be able to help. He called her and asked if he could come over for a few minutes. Marian said she'd be home.

He left his office at two-thirty and drove directly to her place. She was waiting for him.

"Lowell, it's good to see you. Come on in."

It wasn't Oklahoma anymore, but she was dressed in casual Oklahoma. They sat in the living room.

"Marian, tell me about Tony."

Her eyes narrowed.

"Tell you what?"

"What does he do?"

"He's a garbageman."

"That's one way to get around," Lowell quipped.

"It's his way." Marian was chilly.

"Now, Marian, I think that man knows something I need to know."

"I'm sure," she said sarcastically

"Seriously, do you see him?"

"He's living with my sister."

"He really does get around!"

"For some time, now. Listen, Lowell, I'd just as soon not talk about him."

"I have to talk about him," Lowell insisted.

"O.K., then. Be my guest." Marian moved to the couch on which Lowell was sitting. Lowell enjoyed the proximity, as had so many others before him.

"Please, Marian. Be serious a minute."

"Five, if you like, but that's all."

Lowell put his head in his hands as if to force concentration on his business and public duty. "This guy knows something."

"He doesn't know much."

"No, really. He knows something and he has you in some sort of bind. I could see that the first time we talked."

"I tell you, Lowell, the guy doesn't know much, but I do think he's scared. He threatened me last week. Said his pal Rizzo would play tough with me. I don't get it."

"Rizzo? Who's Rizzo?"

"His boss at the garbage company."

"I thought the man's name was Rusto."

"No, Rizzo."

"Harold said Rusto."

"Harold?"

"Yes. I wanted to talk to Tony because I thought he was your husband, so I went to U.P.S.

the other night and asked to see Mr. Fouts. To my surprise, someone whom I'd never seen before came into the office. The fellow said he was Harold Fouts."

"A lot of people have never seen Harold before, and some who have, wish they hadn't."

"He seemed very upset. I asked him if he had children. He said his daughter was six years old. Seems he had some sort of complaint against the garbageman, Tony. He thought I was from the garbage company."

"That's Harold. He's got it in for Tony. Thought Tony was doing something to Mavis. He told me he wanted to get him fired."

"Yes, he said that," agreed Lowell, trying to remember the rest of the conversation. "I thought he mentioned the name of Rusto."

"No, that's Rizzo. Tony works for him. They both moonlight for a couple of goons out of Miami. There's some bimbo in the Mayor's office who works with them, too. And, I'll tell you something, Lowell, but I don't want it to go any further than here. I think they peddle dope."

"Wait a minute, Marian!" He paused for a long minute as if trying to piece these events together.

"What was your donation to the Widows and Orphans Fund?"

"We didn't donate anything. Tony let Rizzo put my name down on that donation. Guess they thought no one would know."

"Someone found out," said Lowell, referring to himself.

"I gave Tony hell. He got mad and left and that's the last I've seen of him. The crumb!"

"You think he's running dope?"

"He's running it for others. I don't think he knows what they are doing. Always has money, though."

"Marian, you have just put your finger on a very big problem. Bigger than I thought." He leaned back and closed his eyes.

Marian thought how peaceful he looked. She thought how wonderful this man Lowell was . . . how strong . . . and, he didn't even know it. Imagine that. Really macho. And he doesn't even know it. She wanted to have him hold her.

Just as she started to make her move, Lowell opened his eyes and sat forward.

"Goddamn it, Marian. This is a dope-and-pay-off case. I was looking for widows who didn't exist."

"For widows?"

"Yep. And orphans. Found the orphans, but no widows. I'll be damned."

Marian hoped not.

"What did you say Tony was doing now?" Lowell inquired.

"Picking up garbage and living with my sister, Leona."

"Evidently, he's picking up some other things as well."

"Seems so."

"Will you call your sister and ask her to talk to me alone?"

"Sure. You want me to get her over here?"

"Yeah, that might be a good idea. Let's do it that way."

Marian went into the kitchen. The hum of one side of the conversation indicated that she had found Leona at home.

Returning to the living room, she said, "Leona will come over now, but she has to bring the kids."

Lowell was mightily burdened with his new-found knowledge.

CHAPTER FIFTY

Leona came over as quickly as she could get the boys ready. As she came into the Fouts' living room, Lowell could see a slight family resemblance. He stood up and Marian introduced them. She then gave her sister a peck on the cheek. The children were glad to see each other and they raced off to the backyard.

"Lowell is an investigator for the government," Marian informed Leona. By putting her arm though his, she also informed her sister that this one was Marian's man.

Looking at Lowell, Leona was impressed. She noticed his firm jaw and good hairline. He had bright eyes and an eager look. When Marian took possession of his arm, he had brighter eyes. He wasn't as tall as Tony, but he was no less athletic. He was to be Marian's. That was clear.

"Yes, Mrs. Remmer, I'm trying to get the facts together on a tax-exempt fund which is managed out of the Mayor's office for widows and orphans."

"You're very thoughtful, Mr. Spisak. But my husband's company was carrying good life insurance on him. Because his death was accidental, the policy pays a great deal more. We're already receiving substantial help."

"I don't think you understand," Spisak started, but Leona was full of information.

"Tony's company has a lawyer and he has told me that we can sue the electric instrument manufacturer for what Tony calls a bundle. It seems that the instrument had a faulty part and the company knew about it. It's generous of you to offer to help us, though. Isn't it, Marian?"

"I think Lowell wants to tell you something else." Marian looked at Lowell who was not far away.

"Yes, Mrs. Remmer . . ." Lowell started.

"Leona," Leona corrected.

"Well, uh, yes, Leona. I've been looking into the Mayor's Fund and we believe it's a phony."

"Oh, I hope not. So many people need it," said sweet Leona.

"That may be, but there is something odd about the way the money gets into the Fund."

"Just so it gets there. That's the important thing."

"Well, that is one way to look at it," Lowell continued. "No, there's something funny about the donors."

"How can you say such a thing when people have been so generous? Although I don't need it, many do. I'm grateful for those people."

"Mrs. Rem . . . Leona, the money doesn't go to the widows and orphans as far as I can see."

"Who gets it, then?"

"It looks like the Mayor gets it, but I have to tie that one down."

Even Marian hadn't heard that. Leona looked at her sister and then at Lowell Spisak.

"You mean, it's a fake?"

"Exactly. And your sister's marked down as a donor of $15,000.00. She didn't even know about the Fund until Tony told her."

"Tony?" Leona was defensive. "He has nothing to do with it."

"He doesn't have much to do with it. Marian tells me that he did tell his boss to put her name down as a donor of one package of money the Fund received. Probably thought she could use it for an income-tax deduction."

"I don't think he had any right to do that, did he, Marian?"

"No, he certainly didn't, Leona."

"I'll have a thing or two to say about that when he gets home."

Lowell walked over to her.

"Don't say anything for now. It's better that way. Your friend is connected in some way. He may be the key. That's what I want to find out, Leona. Marian thinks he's handling dope."

Leona became furious.

"Well, he's not. I'd know it if he was. He's not. He's not that kind of person. Marian, you know that." She turned on her sister.

Marian came back, "I know his friends and they're in dope, I'm sure. I met them on a boat."

"When was that?" Leona was now the investigator.

"A couple of weeks ago, when I was supposed to be in Santa Rosa, we went on this boat ride."

"Marian, what are you saying?"

"I'm saying that Tony's friends are in dope."

Lowell took over. "Leona," he said, "we can't prove yet that these contributions amount to dope-peddling payoffs. For the most part, I think they are, and I'd like to talk to Tony."

"Don't you hurt him," she said anxiously.

"Maybe I can help him." Lowell Spisak, agent for the Federal government in the matter of tax-exempt groups, was beginning to see the light.

Leona finally agreed to help, but asked for at least twenty-four hours to sort things out.

Lowell said good night to Marian and drove Leona home. Marian tidied up the dinner things and went upstairs. She stood a long time in front of her mirror surveying her naked body.

I've got a lot left, she thought almost out loud, and, if that man will have me, I'll give myself to him forever.

She closed her eyes and let her hands caress

her body. She felt sleepy and relaxed. She crawled into bed, slipping under the sheets, without benefit of her pajamas. She had been the tigress. Now she wanted to be the hunted.

CHAPTER FIFTY ONE

Next morning, Tony came in from his work and found Leona in the kitchen where she was preparing a cake for the oven. He gave her a big kiss.

"Let me shower and I'll be right down." He gave her a friendly pat.

"I'll be here, dear," she agreed.

In twenty minutes, he appeared, swathed in a red terry-cloth bathrobe she had bought for him. He was shaved, smelled good, and his hair was all in place

He kissed her again. Longer this time. She pulled away.

"Tony, come in here, dear. I want to talk to you."

She invited him into the living room They sat down on the sofa together.

"Now, what's all this about?" He took her hand.

"Tony, I'm worried."

"Honey, don't be. The company lawyer told me that you were going to be all right."

"Not that, Tony. I'm worried about you."

"Me?"

"Yes, Tony."

"Well, get it over with. What is it?" He was trying to figure out what was bothering Leona. Maybe it was his hair oil. He could change that.

"Don't you like my aftershave?"

"I love it, and, I love you. But, I'm worried about you."

"Yeah?"

"Yes, I am. Marian asked me to talk with a nice man by the name of Mr. Spisak, and I did."

"Spisak? What did he want?" Tony was irritated and thought Harold was after him again. "I told you about that nut Harold making a complaint about me to Rizzo. Now, he's got that guy Spisak after me. I'll beat the hell out of both of them when I catch them."

"Tony, it's not that."

"Not Harold?"

"No, not Harold. It's you and some of your friends."

"Yeah? What's wrong with them?" He was defensive.

"I'm not sure anything's wrong with them, but Mr. Spisak is very concerned."

"The sonofabitch!" And he got up and looked out the window.

"I don't think he is, Tony, and he wants to help you."

Tony turned on her again and said, "Tell him

to meet me at the garage. I'll teach him how to sling the cans."

"Tony, it's not that. It's serious."

He came back to the couch. "Leona, what are you talking about? Serious? Wants to help me? Tell him to get off my back!"

"Tony, I think you'd better talk to him. I don't think you know how close to trouble you are."

"I ain't done nothin'," he whined as he slipped into the real vernacular.

"He didn't say that. Some of your friends have done some terrible things and evidently plan to do some more. He's trying to nip it before it goes any further."

"Nip it, huh? I wonder what he's yakking about."

"Dope, Tony. Dope. And payoffs."

"So what?"

"Somebody's going to jail. I don't want it to be you."

"Leona, I didn't . . ."

"Tony, I know you didn't. But, somebody has. And, you're in the middle. They're going to nail you."

"Goddamn."

"Yes, Tony, goddamn. Tony, I know you and I love you. I want you out of this!"

"That's what Marian said."

"Well, I am saying it now and I think I can help you."

"Leona, baby," he pulled her to him and looked into her face. "Oh, baby, I knew something was wrong. It was too easy."

She kissed him lightly and then seriously. They lay back in each other's arms for a long time.

"Help me, baby."

"I will, darling."

Just then, Bubba ran in from his friend's house.

"Hi, Unca Tony! I was good in cops and robbers."

"I hope I will be, too, Bubba," Tony said quietly, and nodded to Leona.

CHAPTER FIFTY TWO

Friday morning, Winship called Rizzo. He was out of the office and Thelma spoke with her. They had had conversations before and Winship thought that Thelma was more in Rizzo's confidence than she really was.

"Please tell the great man," came from Winship in a voice that made Thelma wince, "that F-day is to be the 23rd. F is for flotilla, honey, in case you don't understand. That gives him a week and a half to get things moving. That is, things have to be ready by then."

"Yes, of course," agreed Thelma not understanding anything Winship had said.

"We will need that big yacht again and I want Mr. Murphy there. Not Harry, just Mr. Murphy "

"I'll tell him, Miss Winship."

"And, tell him this for me, too—the Mayor stands in great need. It seems contributions for the Widows and Orphans Fund have fallen off. He doesn't like that."

Just then, Tony stuck his head in the door.

"Where is Rizzo?" he asked, not seeing that

Thelma was on the telephone. Then he came into the room.

"Yes, yes. I'll ask Mr. Rizzo to call you back. I'll help him to get all this done. Too bad about the Mayor." She hung up.

"What's all that about?" asked Tony, as if it was his business.

"That wonderful Mayor! He's having trouble getting money into the Widows and Orphans Fund. Seems Mr. Rizzo has to dig up some more contributions. Something about business being bad. Anyway, what do you want?"

"Rizzo said he wanted to see me."

"He's not here."

"When will he be back?"

"He should be back by now."

Tony left and bumped into Rizzo in the hallway.

"Hey, Tony. Wanna see you."

They returned to his office and Thelma came in.

"Any calls?" Rizzo inquired.

"Some complaints that I took care of. And, Miss Winship called. Says she needs the yacht on the 23rd and things should be ready."

Rizzo was looking at his mail and not really listening to what she was saying. Finally, it sunk in just as she said, "Yes, and the Mayor says you are slow in your contributions to the Widows and Orphans Fund."

"O.K., O.K., Thelma, great, great." Rizzo tried to shut her up.

She would have none of it.

"Wants you to get Mr. Murphy but not what's his name . . Harry. Just Mr. Murphy ."

"O.K., Thelma. I'll call when I want ya."

She left the room. Tony was looking at the sporting green. "Goddamn it, Tony, we have to make a decent pickup. Don't want the Mayor sore."

"Sure, Mr. Rizzo, sure."

Rizzo turned to his private phone and dialed. Tony could hear three rings. In a low voice, Rizzo said, "We have the stuff. Three hundred big ones."

There was a pause and then he continued, "I have to send a garbage truck out that way to make a special pickup. Guy's name is Tony. He'll say my name. O.K., be there."

Tony took an address on a piece of paper. Rizzo walked over to the big company safe. He opened it and pulled out ten little grey boxes and put them in a shopping bag he had stashed away in the safe.

"O.K., Tony. Take these along. The guy will have a baby-buggy out on the sidewalk. Put the bag in the buggy and pick up a box."

"Got it," snapped Tony, as he left the office. As he passed Thelma, he hissed, "A baby-buggy, yet!"

CHAPTER FIFTY THREE

In the Philippine shipping office, young Loredo was quite excited because he had just been informed through a coded wire that the arrival of the President would be at Noon on the 23rd. He immediately called his friends together for the purpose of arranging a welcoming boat of their own. It would take several of them to decorate it properly. Then there was the question of how their craft was to be used.

Juan Loredo felt that any kind of incident would finish the incumbent Philippine regime and with that he would be called back to heal his wounded country.

Father and son worked long into the night on their preparations. Strategy which had been suggested before now became finalized so that the full advantage could be taken of the moment.

CHAPTER FIFTY FOUR

Leona answered her phone. It was Lowell Spisak.

"Tony's not here now, Mr. Spisak. He called and said he had to do some work for Mr. Rizzo."

"Did he say when he'd be back?"

"No, he didn't, but I think he'll be here around three. He was out very early this morning. He'll be tired."

"Don't say anything. I'll be there at four-thirty."

"Thank you, Mr. Spisak. I hope it works."

Tony was upstairs cleaning up when Spisak arrived. Leona took Lowell into the living room. Then she called Tony. He appeared in his bright Hawaiian shirt.

Spisak was seated on the couch. Leona was in a love seat near the t.v.

"Hi, Tony," Spisak smiled reassuringly.

"Hello, Mr. Spisak." Tony came across the room and joined Leona, draping himself over the arm rest of the love seat. "Leona said you wanted to talk to me. Well, here I am."

Spisak renewed his smile.

"I do. I'm afraid you're mixed up with some bad people."

"That's what Leona says. Marian said it, too."

"Tony, I need your help. I thought I was looking at a tax problem and I guess I am, but there is something else. You can really help."

"I don't know anything about taxes. Just that I have to pay them."

"Some people don't," Spisak smiled again. "Some of your friends, for instance."

"Why don't they?" Tony was trying to find out what Spisak wanted.

"Well, it's a long story. They think they're getting something for nothing. You pay for them, Tony."

"I what?"

"Well, they don't pay. Somebody has to. And some of it falls out of your pay."

"Mr. Rizzo pays his taxes. He was griping about that the other day." Tony tried to remember more about what he had heard.

"Yeah, that Rizzo. I'd like to talk to you about him." Spisak was moving in.

"He's my boss."

"I know. What do you do for him?"

"I handle Route 35."

"Where is that?"

"Mostly Twin Peaks."

"Do they send you to other areas on other routes?"

"Oh, sometimes." Tony moved onto the couch nearer to Spisak. This was man-talk.

"You make garbage pickups or trash?"

"Mostly garbage. But, sometimes trash. Sometimes I get an envelope from a customer. Guess he's paying his bill or something."

"Do you ever give a customer anything?"

"Oh yeah. Some time ago I gave one a new garbage can with a box in it."

"A box?" Spisak leaned forward.

"Yep. This last time there was a box all wrapped up. Then the lady gave me a suitcase. It was heavy. I took it to Rizzo. I thought he'd give it to me when he was finished with it. It would have helped in my moving. But he didn't give it to me."

"Ah . . . Mr. Rizzo . . . do you run errands for him?"

"Yeah, a lotta times."

"Does he give you anything extra?"

"Oh, yeah, he does. I help him a lot. He pays me a C bill, sometimes more. Told me to keep it under my hat."

"Under your hat, huh?"

"Yeah, that's funny, too, 'cause I don't have any hats." He gave his head a little wiggle so that Spisak would notice his hair.

"When you have as good-looking hair as you do, it would be wrong to cover it up with a hat."

"I like it that way."

"Have you made any pickups recently?"

"Today."

"What did you do?"

"Rizzo put ten little boxes in a bag and gave me an address. I was supposed to see a guy wheeling a baby carriage. Imagine that!"

"Did you find him?"

"I always find them. I put the bag in the baby carriage like he told me, and took out a box. There was something funny about that baby carriage."

"Funny, huh? What was that?"

"There was no baby in it."

Leona had kept out of the conversation until this moment.

"Tony, honey, doesn't that tell you something?"

"I did wonder what that man was doing wheeling an empty baby carriage."

"Mr. Spisak, what do you think that man was doing?" asked Leona pointedly.

Lowell looked at both of them and said, "That man was making a pickup. Dope."

"Dope?" questioned Tony. "You know, Marian said something like that. Not the baby carriage . . . dope. I don't use the stuff, Mr. Spisak. I don't."

"Tony, I think you're operating right in the middle of a dope ring. It comes pretty close to City Hall."

"Miss Winship's in City Hall. She went with us on a boat ride."

"Tell me more about the boat ride, Tony. Who else was there?"

"I took Marian and got Millie for Mr. Rizzo. Two men were there from Miami. They were important, Rizzo said. Anyway, we had enough to drink."

"Anybody else?"

"Yeah, like I said. Miss Winship and the two broads the fellows from Miami had."

"Where did the boat go?"

"We just went around. Then the next day— that'd be Sunday— we went in the ocean and then over to Stinson Beach."

"Did you land?"

"Oh, no. We had a picnic on the boat. I'd been to Stinson Beach once before. On the land. Had a steak fry in the park. My girl got sick on the road over. It wasn't much fun."

"Notice anything funny on the boat trip that day?"

"No, I didn't, except that Miss Winship didn't have a date. She didn't seem to mind. She and Mr. Murphy talked a lot to each other."

"Mr. Murphy?"

"He's the big boss, I guess."

"Are you going on any boat rides soon?"

"I don't know. Guess I would if I was asked, and if Leona wants to go."

"If anyone asks you, please tell me, will you?"

"Sure, I will," said Tony.

"Mr. Spisak's our friend, Tony. And we have to help him."

"O.K., Mr. Spisak. If Leona says O.K., then O.K. I'll help you."

He already had.

"One thing, Tony. Please don't mention our talk about taxes or anything else to Mr. Rizzo."

"No, I won't, Mr. Spisak."

"Keep your eyes open and let me know about the boat ride and your special delivery service. I'll call Leona. You tell her. This won't take long once we get started."

"What won't take long, Mr. Spisak?"

"Oh, getting these fellows who should be paying taxes."

"We'll get'em, all right."

Leona and Tony showed Lowell out and closed the door.

"Oh, Tony." Leona put her arms around his waist. "I love you so and I'm so afraid."

Tony leaned down and gave her a reassuring kiss. "Don't worry, honey. I don't know what all this means, but I like Mr. Spisak and I'll help him."

CHAPTER FIFTY FIVE

Lowell Spisak drove over to Marian's with no official thought in mind. She was delighted to see him and was very interested in what had transpired. She was fixing dinner for Mavis and invited him to stay.

Although she missed Tony's contributions to the larder, she turned out a very special meal which, judging from the way Lowell polished it off, must have hit the spot with him.

After dinner, Mavis insisted on being read to. During this procedure, she fell asleep.

When Marian returned to the living room after tucking Mavis into bed, Lowell was watching television.

Marian sat down and watched the end of the program which had interested him.

"Now, that was some dinner for a poor bachelor!" he said, turning off the t.v.

"I'm glad you liked it."

"What's with Mr. Fouts?" Lowell inquired.

"He has a girlfriend and he's leaving me," she replied without expression.

"That's the damnest thing I've ever heard!" Lowell was laughing inside.

"Can you beat it?"

"The guy must be crazy!"

"He may be, but I'm just as glad because there wasn't very much between us anyway. I got pretty sick of his coming in at one o'clock in the morning. Believe it or not, he came home drunk one night."

"It's hard to imagine. What are you going to do?"

"Just sit it out, I guess. He's gone to the YMCA. Isn't that funny? That's where Tony went."

Lowell came over to her and put his arms around her. For once, Marian was not the aggressor.

"Marian, I'll try to help you."

She began to cry. She put her head against his shoulder and bawled.

She shook. He stroked her. She leaned against him and took his nice, clean, white handkerchief, and began to dry her eyes. In all his life he had never seen anything more startlingly beautiful than her glistening eyes. Mascara was running, but that didn't make any difference. She took his handkerchief and patted her face, eyes, and lips. In her subconscious, she worried about the laundry problem. Little did she know that Lowell Spisak planned to enshrine this piece of linen to show to their great-grandchildren

"Oh, Lowell." She looked at the decorated handkerchief. "What a mess. I didn't mean to do that."

"Marian, dearest, relax. You've just been through a couple of damn bad moments. Now, just relax." And he cradled her close to him again. He began to hum a little melody, almost inaudibly. It was loud enough, however, to go straight to her heart.

She raised her eyes to see Lowell looking at her. Then she closed her eyes and offered him her lips. Her invitation was accepted. The moment lasted a lifetime.

Lowell did not return to his office the next morning from his apartment. Taking advantage of a razor Tony had left, he made himself presentable. Marion ironed his shirt for him and he looked as good as new.

CHAPTER FIFTY SIX

Saturday blossomed.

Harold arose from his modest YMCA bed whistling. He put on his glasses and looked at himself in the small mirror which the management provided. He smiled at himself. First with a small smile, then with a big smile. He looked closely at his teeth. Then he brushed his sparse hair. He was ready. Almost ready. He still had to put his clothes on.

His car was parked nearby. He put his meager belongings into it and then drove to Thelma's house. It was seven forty-five a.m. His arrival was earlier than Thelma had planned.

She was fixing some coffee for herself and anticipating all of the joys that the big day would most surely bring her.

Her doorbell rang. She extricated a curler from her hair, hitched her flowered kimono about her, and went to the front door. She opened it eagerly.

There stood "Prince Charming" with a little bundle under his arm.

"Harold! What a nice surprise. Come on in."

"I'm a little early," said Harold coming across the threshold.

"That's all right." Thelma busied herself with his parcel and hat.

"Have you had breakfast?"

"No, I haven't."

"You just come right on in here and we'll take care of that."

Thelma had a more business-like air than Marian. Somehow or other Marian sought to throw things together in a manner that did not secure the future. This lady, though on the brink of fading, seemed to have everything organized.

In the kitchen, Thelma quickly produced a steaming cup of coffee and a maple bear-claw with melted butter.

"Oh, boy, that looks good," Harold observed.

"Tastes even better, Harold." And Thelma gave him an old fashioned serviette. Then she sat opposite Harold, offering him cream and sugar. She then took care of her own cup of coffee.

They smiled across the table at each other in almost perfect contentment.

"Thelma, I have left my wife."

Harold was a direct one once he saw the path.

"That is very sudden, Harold."

"No, not sudden. It started the third day after I married her."

"You poor thing," Thelma whispered and she

went around the table and put her arms around his narrow shoulders.

"Thelma, you are so warm and wonderful."

He felt the softness of her breasts against his shoulders.

He had been holding his coffee cup as he recited this chapter of his life.

Slowly, he put the coffee cup down and as Thelma vibrated against him, he turned in her direction. Her kimono had slipped aside and the beauty of her curving breasts was suggested softly to him.

He tried to control his sudden urge, supressed since childhood, to seek the strength-giving love of mammary contact. He actually shook. She took his head and pressed it to one of her now-naked breasts. His lips sought the life-giving target. She closed her eyes and her head dropped back in ecstasy. His arms encircled her hips, which were thrust inward toward his body.

"Dear love," she whispered, her head now down and her lips caressing his ear.

He drew her closer. She gasped and sighed.

They both lost all sense of time and place.

"Come, darling," she whispered, as his now warm hands traced the beauty of her breasts. She gently raised him from where he sat and kissed his lips until Childe Harold became Great Harry of the Cloth of Gold.

His hunger knew no limit and hers was the will to satiate.

In one small pause they separated long enough for one of her hands to find one of his, and she led him from the kitchen up a short flight of stairs to her sylvan bower, designed by a flaxen-haired princess to arouse sensual feelings of love that somehow, until this moment, had escaped her.

Harold was not really conscious of anything except an internal excitement now visible in the external as well, the likes of which he had not experienced before. Without the sense of it happening, he was being undressed. No great task, but neatly done by urgent hands. He stood finally as Nature had made him. A sight of great beauty to his beholder. And she, no less a sight to him. Her kimono slipped away, her hair had fallen around her face and neck as she stood before him in the half-light of her temple.

There was no shame. There was no guilt. There was no concern for the world's opinion.

Two people amongst the countless number of the earth, stood face to face drinking in the natural differences of the other. No strangers now, they moved toward each other once again. The scene might not have photographed well, but it was a natural coming together, a welding, a fusion in which the actors took on classical proportions. They cared, and the beauty of their care shone brightly, and led them, though blind, to the haven of her spinster bed.

How long they loved and sought the stars or

rolled the clouds apart for a closer view of Heaven is no matter of record, nor did it count, for it was Saturday. The first day of the rest of all the love that was to follow.

Two souls lost, now found. Redeemed. The rage of the storm turned. The winter now became blossoming spring. Night's shadow turned to day's delight.

What happened then has happened before. Twice one-thousand-billion times, or so, as the population of the world can testify.

But here, it was a simple intercourse between the two, turning lost and lonely lives into great reservoirs for future happiness.

And so, Thelma and Harold, two persons condemned to nonexistence, found love and immortality.

The first to speak in normal tones and language was Thelma.

"Thank you, Harold," were her simple words of appreciation.

Harold lay back with closed eyes. "I have taken so much from you, Thelma. How can I ever make it up?"

"There is nothing to make up, Harold. I think we're even," she said quietly.

"I love you, Thelma. I love you."

Without his glasses, he could hardly see her, but it didn't matter. She kissed him and held him to her body. It wasn't exactly the Pieta, but it was close. Contented with a feeling he had not felt before, he rose and found the bathroom. Thelma had discovered the man in him, the man that he always knew was there.

Thelma lay sprawled on her bed. Cleopatra. Madame Recamier. Madame Bovary. Brunhilde. All in one. She had in her life humbled herself for a small taste of maleness. Never satisfied, always guilty, always unhappy, her every effort to be a woman clothed in failure. Now, every part of her body cried out in exaltation to celebrate the triumph. It had tired her physically, but it had lighted a spiritual fire that would warm her for the rest of her life.

This realization, that came to her slowly, gave her a calmness she had never felt before. As she lay there in her bed, she looked slowly around the walls of her bower. Memories of childhood and school life decorated the walls.

Finally, her eyes rested upon a sepia-toned photograph residing in a fancy wooden frame. A smiling man and a serious-faced young woman dressed in white. It was a photograph of the participants in a wedding long ago. The man's hair was short, his collar was high. The bride's hair was long and was held on the top of her head by an obviously complicated combination of hairpins.

Thelma looked at these people. Tears came to her eyes and rolled down her cheeks. She raised her hand for a fraction of a moment in greeting.

"Thanks, Mom and Dad," she said quietly to

herself. She closed her eyes and peacefully went to sleep.

When Harold returned, he saw this vision of a sleeping beauty before him. He tenderly took the coverlet and placed it around and over his love. He then dressed and went downstairs.

He found the back door and descended into the garden. At first, he thought he would pick a bouquet to memorialize the events of the last few hours.

As he chose this flower and then that one and then some greenery, he noticed that the little brick path needed sweeping. Taking the flowers to the kitchen sink where he put them in water, he looked for a garden broom. Finding it, he returned to his chosen garden chore.

One thing led to another and the gardener in Harold became very busy. He trimmed and mulched and swept and collected clippings. He surveyed his work. Just as he was giving himself self-approval, he heard his name called in the tones of a Swiss bell.

"Harold? Harold, you funny man! What are you doing?"

And there she was in a long white and blue kimono. An angel descended.

"Thelma, your garden is beautiful. I picked you a bouquet."

"Yes, I saw it." She came to him and took his hand. "Harold, you sweet thing."

"You and your garden and your home are all magic." Harold was becoming a poet.

"You must be dead from all this work." She surveyed the labors of her master gardener.

When they went into the house, Harold neatly put away the tools which he had used. The sun was about to set and the area was covered with an orange glow which reflected through the windows of the house. He led her to a comfortable love seat and they sat together, his arm cradling her head which rested on his shoulder.

"I wish we could be like this forever," she whispered.

"Forever," he repeated.

She looked at him. "Why not?" she asked.

He smiled. And then his smile faded. "I have no place to take you."

"We have this." Her eyes swept the room.

"Well, I mean . . ." he began. But she put her finger to his lips.

"Why not?" she offered and cuddled close to him again.

"Do you really want me?" He was hopeful for her agreement.

"I do, Harold. Come and live here. You'll be safe."

His heart warmed and he hugged her.

"Thank you, Thelma. I will."

Thelma was overjoyed. Her palace would have a "prince consort."

"Let us have our first dinner." She kissed him and led him to the kitchen. Had they been the Rockefellers or the Getty's, they could not have had a better time at dinner.

All that was needed to be said in either one's life flooded between them. There was much talk of the work in which each was engaged. At last, they talked about Thelma's employer.

"I think Mr. Rizzo is a gangster," she said in the tones of a conspirator.

"He didn't seem very helpful to me." Harold harkened to the interview he had had.

"Well, I took a call for him the other day from City Hall. It seems the Mayor wants Rizzo to increase his contributon to the Widows and Orphans Fund."

"How does Rizzo have anything to do with that?"

"Well, it's certainly not part of the garbage contract."

"Maybe he's on some committee. We have one at U.P.S. for the United Way."

"I don't think this has anything to do with charity. Anyway, they're going to have some sort of big to-do for the Philippine President and they're going to involve all of the private boats in the Bay. Takes place on the 23rd, and Rizzo is supposed to bring his yacht for the Mayor's party. Some big shot from Miami's coming. Name of Murphy."

"I wonder what the deal is?"

"I think he has something to do with the contributions."

They talked on into the night, then, hand-in-hand, they returned to the spinster's bed, metamorphosing it into a connubial couch.

They enjoyed the garden again, and, on Sunday, they enjoyed themselves.

CHAPTER FIFTY SEVEN

Monday, Harold went back to his house to get more of his things and to make his financial arrangements with Marian. He explained that he had been paid on Friday and that on each pay day he'd give Marian enough for the rent and food.

"Thanks a lot, Harold," said Marian, giving serious thought to how she was going to augment this meager contribution.

"I'm going to live with Thelma," he announced to Marian.

"Congratulations."

"Thanks. She's the secretary to Mr. Rizzo at the garbage company, but she doesn't like him. Thinks he's a crook."

Marian almost said something about her impression of George Rizzo, but she didn't. She said instead, "I hope you'll be very happy, Harold."

"She's certainly happy and I am, too."

Marian helped him to pack and load his car.

"I hope that goddamned Tony stays away from Mavis," growled Harold.

"Harold, there's not going to be any more trouble."

"Well, he works for a gangster."

"That may be true."

"Yeah, and they're going to have a big celebration next Saturday. Big deal. Rizzo's going to have some sort of yacht, at least that's what Thelma says. They're all excited about a visit from this President of some damned island in the Pacific. Rizzo's boss from Miami will be there, too. Anyway, Thelma won't have to work on it."

"Oh, how exciting! Now, Harold, you be sure to eat right. You have a sensitive stomach, you know."

Marian's last whack at being a mother to Harold.

"I'll watch it," answered Harold smugly.

Mavis, thinking her father was going back to Oklahoma, kissed him goodbye and went out to play with the neighborhood children.

Harold returned to Thelma's and, with his new key, let himself in. As he entered the house with no Thelma in it, it dawned on him that she worked days. With Thelma, it had not yet sunk in that Harold worked nights. That was going to be a problem. Well, at least they'd have the weekends.

Marian went right to the telephone and called Lowell Spisak. He wasn't in. She left her name and a message that he call her immediately upon his return.

CHAPTER FIFTY EIGHT

Lowell showed up at Marian's about six-thirty. She had just given Mavis her supper. She ran up to him and cried out, "Daddy has left to go back to Oklahoma."

"He has?" puzzled Lowell.

"Yeah. And he took the car."

Marian broke up the conversation and greeted Lowell with a penetrating kiss.

"Sit down, honey and take some weight off your feet. Relax. I'll be down in a few minutes. I have some news for you." And she disappeared with Mavis.

When all was quiet upstairs, Marian returned.

"My husband, or should I say, my lately-departed husband, came back today to pick up his treasures. While he was here, he told me that his girlfriend, Thelma—she works for that creep Rizzo—got a call from City Hall and some damned thing is being planned with the yacht I was on."

"What's that?"

"I said, City Hall is going to use the yacht I

was on in some kind of affair next Saturday. They are meeting the Philippine President. The guy from Miami, Mr. Murphy, is going to be there, too, I guess. I think he's Rizzo's boss in the dope thing."

"Sounds odd to me." Agent Spisak tried to put it all together. Boats. Contributions. Mayor's Office. Miami. The President. Put it all together and it could spell out a big operation.

He was trying to figure out what the President of the Philippines had to do with the case. If the President was in on a delivery, it must be a very big deal.

Then, the Mayor's Office. Contributions to the Widows and Orphans Fund. The involvement of the Mayor was now certain in Spisak's mind. Next Saturday? He referred to his pocket calendar. Saturday was the 23rd.

"Marian, call Leona, will you? I think I should talk to Tony right away."

Tony was home and Spisak left for Leona's, telling Marian he'd be right back.

"What's up, Mr. Spisak?" asked Tony as he and Spisak seated themselves in Leona's kitchen.

"I think a big move is on, Tony. I have just been informed of some activity planned for next Saturday."

"Yeah? Gee, I forgot to tell you! I think maybe Rizzo's going to have another party. He didn't ask me yet "

"Tony, check it out and get back to me right away. We've got to get the narcs in."

"That bad, huh?"

"It's more than widows and orphans, now."

"I'll hang around Rizzo. He'll probably have me do something. Boy, I'd like to get out on that boat again. Guess Rizzo's girlfriend, Millie, would, too."

"Keep your eyes open, Tony. Here are my telephone numbers. Call me or call Marian."

"How's Marian?"

"She seems O.K."

"With you around, I guess she hasn't had time to miss me."

"We have been pretty busy," Spisak admitted with a smile.

Early the next morning, Spisak called City Hall pretending to be a local representative for one of the leading newspapers in Manila and saying that he would like to know the schedule of the President's anticipated visit.

"He will arrive on the twenty-third. Next Saturday," the secretary told him. She thought his ship would pass under the Golden Gate at Noon.

"Yes, he will be given a civic welcome. The St. Francis Yacht Club will be out in full force. Other yacht clubs around the Bay will also be involved."

"Will the Mayor participate himself?"

"Are you kidding? The Mayor is a nut on regattas. Oh, please don't quote that."

"Where will he greet the President? At one of the piers?"

"No, the plan now is for him to meet the President's ship near the St. Francis Yacht Club."

"What happens then?"

"The party goes to Pier 9 and the old riverboat, where Otto Luckner will put on a great lunch for everybody in the official party. Good drinks, great food, and two bands."

"That sounds exciting."

"We hope it will be."

Not long after Spisak's call, someone from the Philippine Bank called and was given the same information which Spisak had just received.

CHAPTER FIFTY NINE

On the other side of town, in his garbage management office, Rizzo had Clemens on his private line.

"Jeez, Clemens, you're our number one guy. What the hell has happened? Are you against kids or something? I gotta see Mr. Murphy at the end of the week. Wanna give him a good report."

"Listen, Rizzo. You're not out there on the street. This new Police Chief . . . he hasn't gotten his orders yet, or, some rookies are trying to play big."

"Look, Clemens, don't give me a lot of bull. Mr. Murphy likes the receipts. He don't care about your problems, so get out there and bust your ass."

"Damnit, I can't help it if there are policemen in every school yard."

"Well, get'em on the way home."

"How do you think I done what I done?"

"Do it some more."

"Listen, Rizzo, stick it!"

"So long, candy man."

CHAPTER SIXTY

At sunset, Millie returned to her spacious Telegraph Hill apartment and was about to wash the grime of the town from her hands and face, when her phone rang. It was George Rizzo.

"Hi, baby," George sidled over the telephone. "What'cha doing?"

"I'm sitting here eating bon bons and looking out at Coit Tower and wishing."

"Wish no more, baby. I'll be there in ten minutes."

"Make it fifteen. I'll put on another face."

"You got it!" and he rang off.

"The little sonofabitch!" she gritted. "Always in a hurry."

In twenty minutes, Rizzo arrived. He drove his car into one of the two garages that went with the apartment.

The place had a small elevator and he went to it. Small was scarcely the word for this piece of equipment. It was a friend-maker. It took less than five seconds to get to know a perfect stranger intimately. On this ride, he had no company. He could expand.

Without the courtesy of ringing her bell, he unlocked Millie's door with his key. Time for that later, he laughed to himself. Sunset highlighted one side of Lillie Coit's monument to what she thought was good about the San Francisco Fire Department.

George Rizzo stepped to the t.v. set and turned it on, at the same time saying, "I'm here, baby!"

"Baby" stepped into the living room as if stepping out of a fine dressing room at I. Magnin's. She walked right up to little George and seized him like a mother bear. Within a matter of moments, George had forgotten the t.v. and was fighting for breath.

"Damn, but you smell good, honey," he gasped, as he was finally able to come up for air.

"Ought to, Georgie," she smiled, smoothing down her gown, which put the upper part of her chest in fine relief. "This gown just came. If you like it, I'll keep it. It's in for only nine hundred bucks."

George took one look at the rest of Millie and decided it was worth it.

"That Parquez guy is going to be at our hotel and everybody is going ape. Seems they have big security problems."

"We'll be on the yacht with him, you know. We changed the plan. He's going to get off his ship with his party and join us aboard the yacht. Then we'll take a swing around the Bay and end up at Luckner's riverboat for luncheon. Won't that be something?"

"Georgie, you're a good little planner." With that, she unzipped something at the side of her gown and stepped out it, naked as the day she was born. But bigger, of course.

George took his coat off, but not his eyes. She plumped a few pillows into shape on the room's low couch and fell into them. George, now attired for the occasion, followed suit.

He was a small man and, when he was not loaded, quite agile. This amused Millie as she never knew from what quarter he would attack next. But attack he did. Millie lost all sense of balance in the onslaught and finally threw back her head in grateful exhaustion.

The attack made, the bastion mounted, the enemy put to flight, the banner secured, the tired chieftain retired to his tent.

Actually, George rose and went to wash his face in the bathroom. When he came back, Millie was smiling like the Mona Lisa.

He went and lay next to her. She couched his head in her ample bosom and purred like a kitten. The sun had completed its day's work and the lights on the hill twinkled.

"George, do you want to go out or shall I fix some soup here?"

"Soup here," he grunted.

And that is what they had. It was obvious that Millie was looking forward to meeting the

President in the Mayor's select company aboard the yacht.

Later George, pleading a heavy day, kissed Millie good night. As the little elevator door closed, he gave her a wink which she returned just as the door made contact with its jamb.

CHAPTER SIXTY ONE

With the early morning City Hall business under control, the Mayor sat at his big desk and rustled some papers. His secretary and Clarissa Winship sat in front of him, pads in hand.

"So, that's the list then," he chirped, as he looked over the list his secretary had given him.

"Who is this Mr. Murphy?" he queried.

"Oh, that's a friend of Mr. Rizzo's. He's a big donor to the Widows and Orphans Fund."

"Ah, yes." The Mayor started to close his eyes. "Glad to have him aboard."

"What do you plan to wear, Mr. Mayor?" Winship wanted to get that part of the protocol straight.

"I think striped trousers would be inappropriate. We should dress in yachting costumes." This was a lucky choice, as the President had suggested through his Consul General the same attire.

"Full dress, yachting," Winship echoed.

"I hope the President doesn't wear his frocked coat."

"We'll inform him of the suggested dress code."

The meeting progressed through all phases of the reception. Someone would have to find out in what manner the President could leave his ship and board the great yacht.

The reception line would consist of the Mayor, the Yacht's Captain, the President and his wife, and the California Chief of Protocol. The San Francisco Protocol Officer would officiate at Luckner's lunch. Drinks and hors d'oeuvres would be served while the yacht proceeded on a short tour of the Bay before landing at Pier 9. The Mayor was beside himself with the excitement of planning the occasion.

Although it was not a subject of this discussion, Winship was trying to plan the moment for the delivery. She was also concerned about how the payoff would be arranged. These purveyors wanted their money up front. Her interest in the payment was the skim for the widows and orphans.

Clarissa said she would call Fred Belding, a leading San Francisco attorney, who was the Yacht Club Commodore, to further develop the flotilla that would be organized to greet the Philippine President and his wife.

It was definitely decided that the President's arrival under the Golden Gate should be at Noon. The tide would be slack at that moment and the transfer from the larger ship to the smaller one could be made easily.

Winship approached the Mayor to say

goodbye. It was her custom to come very close so as to give the old fellow a happy moment. She was almost sadistic in this approach, which, by this time, the Mayor was coming to expect. Not the sadism, but the approach. The pupils of his eyes dilated and Winship did not let him down.

"Oh, thank you, Mr. Mayor," she gushed, hovering over him like a beautiful bird of paradise about to spear a choice morsel.

"Ahh . . . hhh. Thank you, Miss ah . . . hh Winship." He was practically transfixed. If she had touched him, he probably would have collapsed onto the floor.

CHAPTER SIXTY TWO

When Winship returned to her office, Rizzo was on the line. He asked her to come to a meeting which he was having with the yacht Captain. Rizzo told Tony also to attend. At the appropriate moment, they converged on the marina head-quarters. Rizzo had invited a dark-complexioned young man to join the party. He turned out to be the operator of a Boston Whaler.

After drinks had been served by Tony, they proceeded to do business. First, the problem of the Presidential boarding was discussed. It was decided that the reception should take place on the yacht's fantail. As we have seen, this was a spacious after-deck protected by a large and colorful awning. The Presidential party would descend a short staircase ladder from the bigger ship to an over-the-side landing platform level with the yacht's deck.

It was ascertained by Rizzo that the President's ship had a gangway opening at a convenient deck height to accomplish the transfer of the "goods" with the least difficulty.

The President was looking forward to his trip around San Francisco Bay. Winship had picked this up from the correspondence she had received from one of the Presidential aides.

Rizzo now turned to the Captain and said, "We are going to take some baggage aboard. Some Presidential gifts that the Mayor wants secured. Can the bow companion-way be used to accept this stuff?"

"We could do that," agreed the Captain, "or, we can take this material on aft of the wheelhouse. I can have some sailors stand handy to manage it."

"The cruise-ship has two gangways," Rizzo informed them. "The after one will be used by the President and his party. The baggage can come through the forward one. I think it's on the same level. I just hope those two are not that far apart. Winship, will you please check that?"

"I will," she replied. "I think we have a publicity photograph of the ship."

"If we're lucky," Rizzo continued, "it will show the starboard side. Please get me the photo as soon as you can. It will help."

"You'll have it tomorrow morning."

Rizzo thanked her and then turned to the Captain. "Well, Captain, I think that takes care of our business. We'll talk about the photograph as soon as I get it. Just be sure we have the sailors on the bow to help with the bags."

"No problem," responded the Captain and he took his leave taking with him the dark-complexioned Boston Whaler operator. Tony showed them out.

After they had left, Winship asked, "What are we going to do with the shipment once we have it in our hands?"

Rizzo had given this a lot of thought.

"We'll take it along to Pier 9 and there we will leave the party. When it is convenient, the yacht will pull away. The Captain will take his time getting us over to the marina. In the meantime, payment will be made to our friends. Once this is done, they will be put over the side with their loot and returned to San Francisco in the Boston Whaler. Then we'll proceed to the old marina and meet our customers."

Winship was concerned. "Aren't you afraid of hijackers?"

Impatiently, Rizzo responded, "Nobody knows that these fellows will be carrying money. All the boat operator knows is that he's taking some people back to the dock at Fisherman's Wharf. All this will be arranged with him ahead of time."

"I don't mean to be inquisitive," said Winship being inquisitive, "but where is all of this money coming from?"

"That is Mr. Murphy's problem. From what he has said, I think he has already made the arrangements."

Winship was not yet sure. "It seems to me that that amount of money will be very bulky."

"He'll use high denomination bearer-bonds."

"What about the Mayor's Fund?" Winship asked.

"Mr. Murphy has told us he will handle a greeting for the Mayor in cash."

"Just so's I know."

"Don't worry, Clarissa. There will be enough to cover those damn fool cops and a few others as well."

Rizzo turned to Tony, who had just come back into the room. "Do you think you can get one of our big garbage rigs over here on the 23rd, Tony?"

"Sure could, Mr. Rizzo."

"I think we'll use the machine as our 'safe deposit box' for whatever is left over. What do you think about that, Winship?"

Considering the size and value of the shipment, that sounded like a very safe place to Winship. "Having the truck there is a great idea," she said, "in case we have to move it. Never can tell."

"I'll get the truck there, Mr. Rizzo," said Tony. And then, with a note of sadness like that of a little boy being denied an ice cream cone, he added, "That means I can't take the boat ride, doesn't it? But, what the hell? I guess there'll be other boat rides."

"Good, Tony," said Rizzo. Then turning to

Winship, he went on, "I guess that covers all my bases. Just as I said, we can pay off our friends and collect from our own customers. It will balance out very nicely and all in short order."

Winship was concerned about being missed at the luncheon.

"Just tell the Mayor that someone has to watch the store and that you've been elected."

"I think he'll be so jazzed up with all those people he won't know whether I'm there or not." Winship felt better.

"I like the idea of getting the customers over here and getting rid of most of the stuff at one time. And also . . . getting all that money in without running around." Rizzo was giving himself a pat on the back.

"Yeah," agreed Tony. "I like that idea. Sometimes those guys are hard to find."

Rizzo, of course, did not fully appreciate Tony's agreement, as he had not personally made deliveries or pickups for years.

Tony was thinking that Spisak would like that idea, too.

CHAPTER SIXTY THREE

As soon as Tony came home, he called Spisak who said he would come right over. He didn't come alone this time. When he arrived in the living room, he introduced Chief Special Agent Dale Harris.

The appearance of Harris took Leona by surprise. She imagined agents were big, two-fisted, and tough. Dale was none of these.

He was small, quiet, and he looked as if he should be resting in a sanitarium rather than actively being a Chief Special Agent of anything.

They all sat down around the coffee table. Before anyone could say anything, Leona turned to the Chief Special Agent and said firmly, "You know, Tony is in a very difficult spot here. He is risking his life to help you. I hope you recognize this and treat Tony properly when the time comes."

Spisak nodded his head. "That is in the works, only we don't want to be too loud about it yet."

"Lowell is right," agreed the diminutive Dale Harris. "Can't do too much now because we really don't know who the Mayor's friends are."

"Just so it's understood," Leona insisted.

"You have to trust us, Mrs. Remmer." Harris hoped he looked at least trustworthy.

Tony was proud of Leona for the way that she was speaking up for him.

In his simple way, he then related to them all that he had heard. Neither Harris nor Spisak questioned what he said. They just listened. At the end of the recitation, they thanked Tony and said they would be in touch as soon as the plans were made. They said polite goodbyes to Leona and left.

"Tony, you were magnificent!" She gave him a hug. "Imagine remembering all that!"

"Yeah," said Tony. "Rizzo and Winship think I'm helping them. I hope they don't find out."

"Well, they won't. These are terrible people, Tony, selling children that stuff."

With that, they went in and had supper with the boys.

As Tony went off to sleep that night, he thanked his lucky stars for Leona. And then he thanked Leona for Leona. The right way.

CHAPTER SIXTY FOUR

With Tony's information passed along the night before, Spisak and Harris went straight to a strategy meeting with their superiors.

It now appeared that the narcs, although they did not know the source, did have a bundle of information on Rizzo and his network. They had not yet, however, established a line into the Mayor's Office. In fact, they had the Mayor down as a friend of law and order.

Some hints had been passed by adventuresome agents early in the Mayor's administration, but "wiser" heads in the department had put any further conversation involving the Mayor to one side. They were now trying to catch up.

"What's this about a garbage truck? Whoever heard of distributing dope in that kind of a monster?"

Spisak stood his ground. "Well, that's the way it's being done and for the very reason that your question suggests."

Harris told his supervisor, "The driver of the truck is now the source of our information. I may say that to the extent we can, we have checked what he has been telling us and it all washes. His wife, or whatever she is to him, is a very bright lady and she has forced him to play ball. I guess she scared him. Anyway, he's with us all the way. I want to get him cleared and free from prosecution."

The head man took over, "We've done that before and we'll do it for this guy, as long as he pays off."

"I'll tell his wife. It will make her feel a hell of a lot better."

They put up two large maps. One showed San Francisco Bay at the Golden Gate, including the St. Francis Yacht Club and Basin. The other showed the San Rafael sloughs and the location of the abandoned marina.

"I think we should have our own boat out there taking pictures. I want pictures, particularly when they hand over the stuff," the Chief directed. Notes were made.

Spisak added, "I think some telephoto shots should be made of the containers. Good enough to I.D. them later."

"Right on, Spisak," agreed the Chief.

"Our men should be over there at the marina when the stuff comes ashore."

Dale Harris, being small himself, recognized the need for support troops.

There was a good deal of conversation as to when the narcs should close in. It was agreed by all that it would be better to wait until the snow had been picked up by the dealers. That way, there would be a complete round-up. They couldn't pick up the President, and probably would have a good deal of difficulty interfering with his crew. They did not know that Fate was to deal an unexpected hand.

The Chief went into housekeeping details asking, "That garbage vehicle that this man operates, isn't there room in that cab for some of our operatives?"

"I think so," said Spisak. "Generally, the garbagemen ride on the rear of the truck back to the garage, but when it rains I'm sure they must ride inside."

"Good. Then let Tony take some of our men with him and try to fix the cab so that its passengers won't be seen."

Spisak's boss, whose field this was not, was beginning to catch the enthusiasm of the conversation.

"Maybe we should send some of our people in there earlier, like a day ahead."

"That's not a bad thought," the Narc Chief said. "Let's organize a small 'PG&E crew' or a gang to shore up old bulkheads."

His assistant made a note.

"This driver was a find." The Narc Chief finally was affirmative in the direction of Spisak.

Spisak responded, "He saved us a hell of a lot of time and a bunch of trouble."

The Chief said, "There are going to be quite

a lot of people there. What kind of cover does Rizzo have for them?"

Spisak answered, "We checked that. He has a large-sized boathouse. It doesn't look like much, but it is big. I think it could handle fifteen or twenty people."

"What about parking of cars?" the Narc Chief continued. "That's a give-a-way."

"Well, you take an exit ramp and cut underneath the freeway. I'd say there isn't any real parking problem. Twenty or thirty cars wouldn't be that noticeable. Also, there is a short-order dive down there that serves drinks. Francita's or something. I think on weekends it does a pretty good business. There would be enough going on down there so that the cars wouldn't be too noticeable."

Dale Harris said, "We don't want any civilian interference. So, if the going gets noisy, we should have a detail there to handle the civilians in the area."

Again, notes were made.

The Narc Chief asked some questions about the time of arrival. They tried to figure out how fast the yacht would make the marina once it left Pier 9.

Lowell Spisak was quick at these calculations. "I make it that if the yacht can get away from the Pier at one forty-five, it should take them a good hour to get to the marina. We should see them shortly after three."

"The luncheon crowd will still be at the old marina," the Narc Chief observed.

"Can't do anything about that."

The Narc Director became expansive. "This may be the biggest haul we've ever had on the West Coast. Maybe anywhere." He could see his commendation now. As he was nearing retirement, this would be very pleasant for him.

Harris was worried about internal security. He suggested that no information as to the operation be passed on to anyone. Certainly not to any of the police departments. They could be helpful, but they should be called in at the last moment. Same with the Highway Patrol.

The Mayor was going to be in for one of the biggest surprises of his little life. They hoped.

CHAPTER SIXTY FIVE

The narcs and the tax officials weren't the only ones having a meeting.

Mr. Murphy arrived in town and set himself up at the Huntington. That evening, Winship and Rizzo went to meet him.

"Say, George. Your last school report was down a little, I noticed. What happened?"

"Well, we had a little breakdown in communications with the police department," explained Rizzo.

"Please get it straightened out. It may cost something, but do it. Now, about this business on Saturday. I've got three big buyers lined up. They will probably buy something more than half of whatever we get."

"Have they paid yet?" asked Winship smartly.

"Oh yes, they have. What they paid is just about what we will have to pay to cover the whole shipment," Mr. Murphy explained.

"The President's man is General Ferreri," Mr. Murphy went on. "Ferreri will have three Lieutenants with him. They will accompany the shipment until they are paid. Where have you planned to take care of that?" Mr. Murphy inquired.

Winship quickly explained how payment would be made on the yacht.

Mr. Murphy looked over at Rizzo. "How much of this stuff are you going to get rid of at the marina?"

"I have my contacts," Rizzo said, "and they want to play. I don't know exactly, but we'll all go away happy I'm sure."

Winship had the economics down pat. "We're going to pay about twelve-million for sixty million on the street."

"Then we got the money, no sweat," sleazed Rizzo, looking over at Mr. Murphy.

Mr. Murphy, the Bishop who always has his extra fund for rainy days, said, "I can touch more if we need it."

They understood that what was going to happen on the yacht would mean some fast work in all of the cabins checking the stuff out. The money problem was not going to be too difficult, as Mr. Murphy again informed them that they would be dealing in bearer-instruments.

Everyone agreed that completing this transaction on the yacht was preferable to trying to do it at the marina.

"I like it," said Mr. Murphy. "We dump the Royal party at Pier 9 and depart after our fond farewells to the President and the Mayor. This will make it easier for our host, Mr. Linker."

"Mr. Luckner," corrected Winship. "We'll invite him to be on-board when we pick up the President."

"Well, tell him he doesn't need to plan luncheon for us," added Mr. Murphy.

Rizzo explained, "We'll have the big Boston Whaler trailing us so that when the deal is done, they can go ashore."

"Good idea," said Mr. Murphy.

A waiter came into the suite summoned by Mr. Murphy's secretary, on a signal from him. Drinks were ordered.

Rizzo sat looking out of the window at the lights in the distance. Mentions of large sums of money had stimulated his lust and he was figuring to himself how he might beat the game. He was thinking these larcenous thoughts right in front of his partners and he was smiling at both of them.

Before the time came to say good night, Mr. Murphy suggested that Winship contact Ferreri and fill him in. This could be done using the prearranged code over ship-to-shore telephone.

Rizzo dropped Winship at her apartment and then went along to see Millie.

During a respite in his pursuit of happiness, he asked Millie if her passport was valid.

"I think it is," she responded. "What do you have in mind?"

"Well, I may want to take a little trip and

it would be nice if you went along with me."

"I'll go, I'll go!" Millie jumped out of bed and danced around with one of the pillows.

Rizzo laughed. She was a great girl. Great sense of humor.

CHAPTER SIXTY SIX

Out in the ocean, aboard the Presidential ship, it appeared that the President and his wife were having a fine rest. Early Saturday morning, the 23rd, he was padding around his ample cabin in his bare feet. His wife told him to put his slippers on. He did.

Elsewhere on the ship, General Ferreri was having a rubdown administered by one of his henchmen, while two others stood by as they discussed their arrival in San Francisco.

"They're expecting the shipment in suitcases," Ferreri announced in between exhalations of breath.

"Yes, and they are ready," came the response.

"They have a yacht which they will bring along side and we will go aboard. You fellows will see to it that the suitcases are delivered out of gangway number two."

"Payment will be made on the yacht?" asked one of the henchmen.

"Oh, yes, the deal will be complete."

"How many of us go with the President?"

"One of you will stick with him. Two of you will stay on the yacht to receive the suitcases and the payment. Arrangements are being made to bring us back to town once the payment is made. By the way, how many cases did you finally put together?"

"Six, General."

"Good."

By the time that conversation had ended, the President was in his oversized bathtub, humming a hill song of his native province.

His wife, who had preceded him in the tub, was now dry and smiling. She approached a porthole with her towel and, on her tiptoes, looked out across the water to see the distant coast of California.

"Francesco, I see land!" she announced to her husband.

There was a splashing in the tub as the President rolled around in complete enjoyment of the warm water. Then he crawled out and began to towel himself. He walked over to the porthole and joined his wife looking out at the distant Golden Gate.

The President's wife looked over at her unclothed husband.

"Really, Francesco. You must not eat so much and you must get more exercise."

He then looked at her and said, "Ah, my dear, and you must eat more. As to exercise, I will

give you some right now." And he made as if
to chase her into the bedroom. She laughed and
told him she had an appointment with her hairdresser in five minutes. That ended the chase.

CHAPTER SIXTY SEVEN

In San Francisco, the weather gave no indication of what the events of the day would bring other than joy. People yawned themselves into the newly born day as if it was to be like any other Saturday. That is, most people. Those involved with the arrival of the President awoke with the adrenalin already in place.

At the St. Francis Yacht Basin, shortly after ten on Saturday morning, Commodore Fred Belding was supervising the placing of flags on his Stephens 52. His guests aboard would be some of the Consular Corps officials and the Chief of Protocol of San Francisco. This element of the government had insisted that he attend the regatta on the Commodore's yacht so that he could make the earlier arrival at Pier 9 where he would act as host for Luckner's luncheon.

Clarissa Winship returned to her apartment from her Saturday morning session with her hairdresser. She had chosen a smart Navy-styled outfit: a brass-buttoned blue coat, with a full white, pleated skirt, topped off with a chic sailor hat. The Mayor's secretary would drive by with one of the Mayor's chauffeurs. They would then go to George Rizzo's yacht.

Leona prepared breakfast for the boys with a prayer in her heart that all would be safe and, that by sundown, Tony would be safe.

"I'll take the boys to the parking lot in the marina near the Presidio so that they'll be able to hear the excitement and the Army salutes. We'll have a picnic.

"They'll love it," enthused Tony.

"Maybe Marian and Mavis will go with us."

"Great."

"How close will the Mayor's yacht be? Will we be able to see the people?"

"I don't think it will be very close. There'll be lots of boats all around."

Tony was to report to his garage about ten-thirty, where he was to pick up his M-1 truck and drive it to a rendezvous at the Presidio. He was taking the big rig because it had power steering and a capacity for three men in addition to the driver.

Mr. Murphy, having spent an active night with Candy, his present "Mrs. Murphy," crawled out of bed and looked at his watch. Even in his pajamas, he looked like a professor.

"Come on, Candy, up and at'em!" And with an unceremonious jerk of the covers, he uncovered a sleepy and somewhat startled nude young woman of twenty-three.

"Oh, Mr. Murphy," she squealed and hopped out of bed. She went to the dressing table and started feeling around for her contact lenses.

Marian had risen with Lowell earlier than all the rest. Lowell departed in dawn's early light for his rendezvous with the narcs, assuring Marian that everything would be all right.

Leona called Marian and suggested that they all go to the marina for a picnic luncheon to view the activities. At first, Marian, not really wishing to see the yacht again, was negative. But, with a few more encouraging words from Leona, she agreed.

Rizzo spent his evening with his wife at home.

He claimed a headache and retired early. Inviting his wife to come along the next day on a boat ride, and knowing she would decline, he left the apartment alone the next morning for Pier 9.

The little Mayor woke up in an excited state, performed his bathroom duties, and called in his aide, who was his valet-chauffeur A choice was made of the proper clothing, including a hat designed for an Admiral of the Fleet.

"Have to be careful with this one," Belpierre chortled. "The seamen may look to me for orders and this would irritate the real Captain! Anyway, I look good in this hat, don't I?"

"Yes, sir, Mr. Mayor . . . I mean, 'Admiral.'" They both laughed.

Thelma shook herself awake and checked the other side of her bed. He was still there. Prince Charming was still there! He rolled over and she kissed him. His eyes flickered, first with the fear born of other days, then immediately with recognition of love.

"Come, my dear, I'll make you breakfast."

"I'd rather just lie here," Harold drowsed.

And, they did. For more than hour they reveled in their mutual proximity.

Finally, hunger took over and dictated a move in the direction of the kitchen.

"I'd sure like to see that yacht of Rizzo's," suggested Thelma over her toast.

"We can see the old tub, if you want," agreed Harold.

And so they made plans for later in the morning. They chose an area near the St. Francis Yacht Club as their target.

CHAPTER SIXTY EIGHT

Rizzo arrived at the yacht mooring by himself. Sailors were working around adding last minute touches. He checked the ward room and was pleased to see that the caterers were in the process of doing their job.

When he saw the Captain, he asked to be shown the hatch down which the shipment would pass. When he saw the companionway to be used, he chose to save Cabin #2 to receive the shipment. He put its key in his pocket.

Tony drove his rig right to the Presidio and proceeded to the main garage in the shadow of the Golden Gate Bridge at the west end of what used to be Crissy Field. There he found Dale Harris, the diminuitive narcotics agent, who was with five of his men. They smiled when they saw the size of the great garbage compactor.

Three of the agents would go with Tony, while the others would proceed with Dale Harris to the Coast Guard Station, where a fast cutter disguised as an old yacht awaited them.

Lowell, having checked with the other agents in Marin, arrived back in time to join Harris on the cutter.

Two "emergency" work crews were laboring in the old marina area. The agents working on the bulkhead became familiar enough with the area to qualify as Army Engineers. The "PG&E" group were running wires and making busy-work installing what looked like a large transformer near Francita's hangout. The gang provided her with some additional coffee and doughnut business.

Leona and Marian, with their children, arrived at the Yacht Club parking lot a little after eleven. The place was already filling up.

Not long afterward, Thelma and Harold parked their dilapidated vehicle not far away.

As Leona and Marian, with the children, were walking to the little beach, Mavis saw her father's car

"Mommie, there's Daddy's car!" And she pointed, just as Harold opened his door and ran around to help Thelma out.

"I wonder where he learned that," Marian thought.

"There's Daddy!" Mavis was excited and loud.

By this time, Leona's attention had been

attracted. The boys had gone ahead to the beach.

"Well, what do you know!" exclaimed Leona.

Marian just watched: first amused, then as the wounded party, then disgusted, and finally with a what-the-hell attitude.

Thelma and Harold, oblivious of the others, took their picnic basket toward the small, but architecturally-decorative, sewage treatment plant where they found a protected place on the surrounding lawn to sit.

Mavis lost them in the crowd.

Tony took the crew aboard the large garbage vehicle and the trip to Marin County began. The men all fit into their places with no trouble. They crossed the new Golden Gate Bridge without incident. (See *Ransom of the Golden Bridge,* by Proctor Jones, Proctor Jones Publishing Company, San Francisco, CA, 1983, for a story of criminal confrontation which had made reconstruction of the Bridge necessary several years earlier.)

Along Highway 101 they traveled, much to the concern and interest of other drivers, unaccustomed to seeing such a large garbage truck in use on Saturday, particularly on such a festive day as this.

Just after Tony turned off the highway, he pulled the behemoth into the shadows of the overpass. The narcs, having found ample overgrowth to disguise their presence, could not be seen. Using their powerful field telephone, they had established contact with Harris on his craft. He told them to stay under cover.

CHAPTER SIXTY NINE

The Chief of Protocol of San Francisco arrived at Commodore Fred Belding's berth at the San Francisco Yacht Club Basin and took his little dog, Patsy, aboard. Belding found him a comfortable chair on the afterdeck. The Protocol Chief was early, as was his habit. A very thoughtful man, he never wanted to keep anyone waiting.

"It's not polite to be late," he always smiled when his habit was noticed.

Shortly after he arrived, the group from the Philippine Consulate arrived with their wives and two of their children.

The children were immediately provided with life jackets.

The Protocol Chief's little dog had a very small life jacket, specially built, which she was already wearing. The children followed suit cheerfully.

His Excellency, the President, in full Naval regalia, accompanied by his petite wife, stood on the bridge of their ship and watched as it approached the Golden Gate.

Hundreds of small motorcraft and sailboats surged toward the President's ship. Although quite a distance from his welcomers, he saluted and waved. He did this for the benefit of those who had picked him out in their binoculars.

The Mayor and his burgee, high on Rizzo's yardarm, were being propelled to this great meeting. It wasn't Queen Elizabeth, whose Bay entry on an earlier occasion had been cancelled due to foul weather, but it was going to be a great meeting nonetheless.

Mr. Murphy motioned to Rizzo to join him. "Rizzo," he said confidentially, "please carry some of this load." Mr. Murphy then gave Rizzo two large envelopes which he, with some difficulty, put into his two breast pockets.

Rizzo was now the sole possessor of more than half of the payment.

Mr. Murphy figured that Rizzo couldn't go anywhere. His own suit took on its original tailored line. Candy, without knowledge of the contents of the envelopes, put another envelope into her big tote-bag.

The group in the reception line had been joined by the Chief of Protocol of California and his wife. He was a genial and open-handed man who made everyone feel that they were in the right place at the right time. He congratulated the Mayor on the enormous activity that was surrounding him.

And, what a display was before them!

Fireboats spraying on all sides, hundreds and hundreds of small yachts, motorboats, sailboats, and several very large ships. There was no prescribed traffic pattern. Flags, sails, windsurfers, motorboats, all going in every direction. It was calm enough and there was a pleasant but not demanding breeze. Slack tide made progress controllable without the necessity of having to correct for tidal drift.

CHAPTER SEVENTY

On the shore, the children of Marian and Leona dove into the picnic basket.

Mavis was concerned as to why her father's car was there. Marian did not answer her directly as she had never given this type of situation any thought.

Having eaten all that they thought they needed, the children ran off again to play on the small beach, hardly conscious of what was going on before them. Mavis heard a bugle sound some military instructions and she looked up. She looked straight up at the profile of her father.

She looked again and, recognizing his glasses and weak chin, she ran to him.

"Daddy, Daddy! I thought you were in Oklahoma."

Harold's disbelief turned to belief.

"Oh, uh, hello Mavis. What are you doing here?"

"We have come to see the boats that Unca Tony has for us."

"What did the little girl say?" Thelma leaned over the picnic basket.

"Oh, Thelma. This is my daughter, Mavis. Mavis, this is Aunt Thelma."

Mavis lowered her head, but her eyes looked up at this new lady. Her father put his arm around his daughter to draw her nearer, but she resisted.

"She's a nice little girl, Harold." Thelma smiled at Mavis and Mavis began to warm to her.

"She's like Marian," said Harold, without generosity or chivalry.

"Here, dear, have a little cookie."

"No thanks. I have to go back to Mommie now."

With that, she turned and, forgetting Bubba and his brother, ran around clumps of people until she found Marian.

"Daddy's here . . . with a lady."

"Isn't that nice, dear. He must have come back from Oklahoma for a little while."

At the sewage treatment plant, Thelma observed, "Harold, she's a pretty little girl."

Harold's eyes narrowed. "What did she say about Tony and the boats?" he inquired.

"She probably picked up from someone that Tony is helping Rizzo handle the Mayor's boat."

"That goddamned Tony. He's still around . . ."

"He's what, dear?"

"Oh, forget it. Let's go home."

"If you want to, Harold," Thelma agreed and began to get ready.

"I do." And he swooped up some of the picnic utensils and dumped them into the basket.

CHAPTER SEVENTY ONE

The Philippine cruise ship, in full flower of flags and banners, sailed under the Golden Gate Bridge. People were throwing flower petals over the railings to the President. These flowers had been well organized. There were thousands of them being dumped from green plastic bags.

Badly timed, someone dumped a bag of garbage.

In falling, the garbage separated and splattered over the stern superstructure of the cruise ship. It could have dropped in the President's face. However, only the deckhand with his swabbing mop noticed the botanical difference.

This untimely delivery was a harbinger, and not of spring.

The yacht bearing the local dignitaries swung into position well off the St. Francis Yacht Club and its waving banners. It came about and headed east, at which time the Captain cut all forward speed in an endeavor to hold the craft steady in the water.

Rizzo, standing near the rail, noted that his

dark-complexioned pilot on the Whaler had positioned himself off the yacht's stern. George raised his hand in greeting. The pilot responded with his.

Slowly, the President's ship passed the Coast Guard Station and began crossing in front of the Presidio.

Just as Harold had completed putting the remnants of their interrupted lunch into their picnic basket, cannons started to go off in the Presidio. He was startled, but then went ahead with his clean-up efforts.

"Don't you want to see what happens?" Thelma asked softly.

By this time, they were standing.

"I don't care, but if you want to stay a moment, I will."

They turned their gaze to the myriad of boats and saw the President's ship approaching Rizzo's yacht.

"Mr. Rizzo must be real excited," Thelma said as she watched.

"Yeah, and Tony, too."

Marian and Leona, along with Mavis, now joined the smaller children on the beach. They were transfixed by the noise and excitement. Navy planes swooping past added to the confusion. Bubba was not bothered, but Harvey was scared. His mother comforted him.

As the cannons boomed, the two ships came

parallel. The yacht was landward of the President's cruise ship.

There was a little jockeying and the two ships came very close. As the yacht was considerably smaller than the ship, people on the shore could see most of what was happening on the starboard rail of the yacht and some of the cruise ship, but they could not see the boarding preparations or the gangplank. This procedure would take place between the two vessels.

Officers on the bridge of each ship could be seen gesturing. Ropes were thrown.

The Captain of the yacht ordered the platform lowered in place at the same time that steps were lowered from gangway number one. Gangway number two was pushed open and heads could be seen poking out to see what progress was being made.

The President's party was waiting patiently, occasionally peering out of the gangway.

At last the order came. Some young officers went down the gangplank first. It was sound. They stationed themselves at the platform landing between the two ships.

The President stepped forward, saluted the flag at the stern of his ship, and heavily descended, followed by his wife. As they came onto the deck of the yacht from the platform, he saluted the American flag. Then he came aboard.

He saluted the Captain and put out his fat hand to greet the Mayor and the members of the welcoming party. He then turned and presented his wife, and General Ferreri, who looked like a dressed-up parrot.

As the whole party came aboard, they moved to the fantail of the yacht and now could be seen by the people on the land.

At the yacht's bow, three sailors were struggling with six large suitcases being lowered carefully from gangway number two.

What was not noticed by anyone on either ship, and probably not by anyone sailing around in the proximity of the two vessels, was a sleek, dark boat, flying the Philippine flag, which came directly along the north, or Bay side, of the President's ship. This craft could not be observed from the land. It stopped for a count of at least five, and then quickly moved away. Within seconds, the water around the President's ship was seen to whiten and writhe at the same time that a fearful explosion took place.

Some thought that it was the continuation of the cannonading from the Presidio. The President's ship immediately listed to the port, so that it was obvious that something very damaging had happened to it.

The yacht's Captain, not knowing what had happened but seeing the almost immediate and precipitous list of the larger vessel, ordered the ropes between the two ships cut.

Rizzo had been knocked down. Dazed for a moment, he rose and looked around for Millie.

Finding her under a chair, he pulled her to her feet and clutching one of her arms, pushed her in front of him along the narrow deck to the bow.

As he did so, he flagged the Captain of the Boston Whaler, not yet affected by the explosion, to approach. He lunged through the sailors who had just completed getting the six bags on deck. He directed them to lower the bags onto the Whaler, which had been thrown a line by one of the sailors on deck. The Whaler was about six feet below the deck on which Rizzo stood. He yelled at Millie to go over the side. She looked down and, in her fright, nearly threw up.

"Go over!" he yelled, and she did, into the arms of a waiting sailor below.

Then Rizzo turned his attention to the bags. They had to be carried from one side of the bow to the other. He tore at one and lowered it to the Captain of the Whaler. As he did so, he motioned to the other two men on the yacht deck to do the same thing. Thus, all six bags were made secure on the Whaler's deck.

Just as Rizzo went over the side, there was another terrible explosion. He yelled at the Whaler's skipper to get the hell out. Two persons tried to follow, but they were too late. One fell screaming into the water.

CHAPTER SEVENTY TWO

Harold, at the sewage treatment plant, in the process of folding the beach rug they had brought with them, turned around for just a second as they were leaving and, in that instant, saw the white water. In the next, his sun hat and glasses were blown off. Every window in the St. Francis Yacht Club followed the glasses. Thelma's eyes were on a whole group of sailboats which flattened-out in the water as if the same hand pushed them over. She saw Harold's glasses going through the air and followed them.

Lowell, on the heavy Coast Guard cutter, was looking through his long-range camera lens and had just photographed the last suitcase being put in place. Now the bags were all lined up near the rail as if they were ready to be removed someplace else.

He turned to tell Dale that he had spotted the bags. By the time that the Narc Chief could get his binoculars in position, the bags had been lowered hastily into the Boston Whaler.

Lowell raised his camera for another shot and

at the same instant saw the white water, heard the explosion, and felt the water rise under his own craft.

The yacht and what was left of the President's ship seemed to separate. The big ship was listing with its port deck nearly meeting the waters of the Bay. It had come around in the water so that its stern faced the Presidio.

Brave sailors tried to do the right thing, but were ordered by their Captain to abandon ship. And, just in time, too, as the great ship shuddered and convulsed in a second horrendous explosion. Its boilers had had all they could take.

With scarcely a whish, the beautiful, wounded cruise ship slipped below the cover of the Bay, its sailors and Captain being rescued by agile Yacht Club skippers.

Otto Luckner had brought one of his specially designed ship-to-shore radio telephones aboard the yacht, to indicate to his staff when the yacht would arrive at Pier 9, so that the champagne could be opened and the steaks made ready for the barbecue. He seized his clever instrument and dialed his secretary, Debbie, who was waiting to hear from him.

"There's been an accident!" he cried into the mouthpiece. "The luncheon is cancelled! I don't know where we will be ordered to go, but I should think it will be the Alameda Naval Air Station. Call Ishi Limousine and have them alert their drivers. I'll contact you in a few minutes when I see what is going happen."

He looked around at the chaos in the water as the sailors were being picked up. There was nothing more to say over the phone, so he just said, "Over and out." He had watched movies closely enough to say it calmly. Of course, that was his nature anyway.

The chaos in the water was nothing compared with the chaos on-board. The Captain, who at the first sign of trouble regained the wheel house, brought his yacht around. Satisfied that the sailors in the water were being taken care of, he steered straight for the moorings of the Alameda Naval Air Station, full speed ahead. There would be some protection there.

The attackers had somehow come upon Winship's first plan and had thought the party was aboard the cruise ship. They left the scene so quickly and they had approached it so furtively that they had no idea that the transfer had taken place.

And, lucky this was for most of the people aboard the yacht. Most, that is, with the exception of Clarissa Winship and the Mayor's secretary. They had been down in cabin number three. Clarissa was in the head when the explosion threw her against the sharp projecting parts of the metal tank fixture. She was literally nailed. As her cerebellum was involved, her release from official duty came without realization or pain.

The Mayor's secretary broke her leg falling against a heavy desk and lay helpless until one of the Mayor's staff sent to find Winship, found them. The Mayor absorbed the shock by being thrown to his knees, during which his gaudy hat fell to the deck. He retrieved it like a rat terrier and then looked around with surprise to see what had happened.

Mr. Murphy and Candy, who had been standing next to the ward room bulkhead, had been able to grab a railing. He had steadied her and although they were off-balance, they had not been knocked down.

The heavy President, in falling, had tripped over a chair and descended on the top of the wife of the Chief of Protocol of the State of California. Fortunately for her, several onlookers, regaining their feet, had rushed forward quickly to disengage the President. His own wife had nearly been blown over the side of the yacht. Shaking and bruised, the President and his wife were hurried to cabin one.

Of General Ferreri, there was no trace.

Marian and Leona were on the beach with the children when they noticed the white water. The explosion brought them all together. The children were terrified and clung to their mothers. Leona was the first to realize what had happened. Frightened though she was, she had the assurance of knowing that Tony should be at the old marina. She prayed intently that the plans had not been changed.

Marian did not know where on the Bay Lowell was supposed to be. She knew for some reason that he would not be on the yacht because she remembered his talking about the pictures he wanted to get.

CHAPTER SEVENTY THREE

The fast motorboat bearing Rizzo and the treasure picked its way through capsized sailboats and well-meaning small motor craft rushing to the assistance of those people still in the water.

As the Whaler cleared all of this, the pilot let both motors go full blast. The speeding boat literally lifted out of the water and planed.

After his spate of instructions to the dark-complexioned operator, Rizzo looked around and was surprised to see a man in a parrot-colored uniform sitting in the stern. He was a dark man with heavy black eyebrows. He looked very serious.

"General Ferreri?" Rizzo cried.

"We are at each other's service." The General smiled and showed a mixture of gold and black teeth.

"Sonofabitch!" Rizzo exclaimed. "You are goddamned lucky!"

"You are very lucky." Ferreri nodded to the cases.

The fast little boat was making a great deal

of noise, and conversation, except for the most basic words, was difficult to understand.

As between Rizzo and Ferreri, however, there was innate understanding, notwithstanding the conference problem.

"That goddamned Tony better be in place," Rizzo thought. He tried to shelter Millie from the spray and wind. When he felt her damp condition, he began to worry about the bags secured forward. Then he concerned himself with Ferreri. Rizzo thought of cold-cocking and dumping him.

From Ferreri's worried look, he was probably thinking along similar lines. However, before these random thoughts could be put into action, the Whaler rounded the slough and began to slam against the water. The pilot reduced his speed.

The Coast Guard cutter carrying the diminutive Mr. Harris and the anxious Mr. Spisak joined the rescue operation, rushing forward to the yacht's assistance. The cutter careened without warning trying to prevent a collision with a sleek black boat coming at great speed across its path. It didn't make it. The cutter went right through it. There were two small explosions and the black boat disappeared without a trace.

Several sailboats were down right in front of them. The cutter wove its way through them.

"What kind of a damn fool is that, plowing through those sailboats at that rate of speed?" yelled Spisak, turning in time to see the two flashes which finished off the black speedboat. The last thing he saw of it as it disappeared under the water was the Philippine flag.

A general movement of small craft toward the two large vessels continued. As Spisak watched, the bigger one was listing dangerously and about to go under. Lowell Spisak noticed that people were trying to get off the yacht.

Just then, the boilers blew on the big ship and its sailors began jumping into the water. The yacht, having cut its rope, changed position and Spisak thought an attempt should be made to save lives, to tow the yacht, to grab the suitcases!

It was not easy passing between the wallowing sailboats, whose crews were making valiant efforts to right their crafts. Smaller motorcrafts were trying to be helpful to the sailors who had leapt from the President's ship.

As this turmoil was making its impression on Lowell, the yacht swung around and high-tailed it to the east. Spisak had a hasty conference with Dale Harris. They decided to follow the yacht. In the excitement, they completely missed seeing the speeding Boston Whaler.

The Captain of the yacht made for Alameda. The Port was ready for him and his load of passengers. Luckner made further contact with his secretary on his special telephone. Cars from Ishi and one other garage were speeding to the Alameda dock with police escort.

The Mayor was beside himself when he heard what had happened to Clarissa Winship. He was also informed that his secretary had broken her left leg below the knee and that one of the crew had made a heavy splint for her.

The President and his shaking wife stayed in cabin one. He was beginning to have reservations about diplomatic receptions in San Francisco.

Mr. Murphy and Candy remained on deck. He did not know where Rizzo's marina was or how to contact him. He was frustrated and had the feeling that except for the envelope in Candy's tote-bag, he was going to lose this one.

By the time the yacht arrived at the Alameda dock, Mr. Ishi and his fleet of limousines had pulled into place. A banged-up crew of people disembarked.

The Mayor, although limping, saw to it that his secretary received ambulance care. He also saw that the body of poor Winship was sent off to the morgue of the City and County of San Francisco.

Mr. Murphy and Candy were taken back to the Huntington Hotel to await a phone call that would never come.

The President and his wife were whisked back to San Francisco with a loud police escort.

When Spisak and Harris found out that Rizzo was not aboard the yacht, they checked with the cutter's Captain over the Bay chart. Spisak had received directions from Tony on how to approach the marina hide-out by land. Finding the spot on the charts was not easy. Fast though events had seemed to move, two hours had ticked themselves away since the explosion.

Harris and Spisak left the cutter. As there was still one limousine available, they commandeered it, feeling that they could approach the marina to better advantage over land.

From the speeding Whaler, Rizzo looked ahead. He saw the balustraded roof of the boathouse. They were nearly there. He motioned the sailor to come back to the wheel, then he yelled his orders to the dark-faced operator and his assistant.

"When we dock," he instructed, "you will see a big garbage truck. Take these suitcases to it. My driver will help you. He knows what to do. Put them in the rear of the machine."

Then he looked over at "parrot-coat."

"Listen," he yelled over the now-subsiding motors, "these sailors are going to dump the bags in a big machine that is parked near the dock."

"No, I want a car! I want to take this stuff back to San Francisco," Ferreri yelled.

"Listen, General, be patient. We'll have buyers

here this afternoon. We'll get the rest of the money. I have most of it already."

Mr. Murphy's vanity and the concern for his Italian-tailored threads had seen to that.

They were now at the marina entrance. There was the boathouse. There was the truck.

CHAPTER SEVENTY FOUR

After the explosion, Marian and Leona thought it would be best to get home and they led the now-excited children back to where their car was parked. They were just loading up when Marian looked across some of the cars near their own and saw Harold and Thelma. They were already in the car. The car would not start. He was looking around helplessly. Just then he spotted Marian. Thelma had no inkling of what was about to happen.

Harold, still in the habit of either blaming Marian for his visitations, or leaning on her to save him, motioned to her for help.

Marian told Leona to hold the kids for a moment. She went over to Harold's crate. By this time Thelma was aware of the fact that Marian was on her way to assist them.

"The goddamned car won't start, Marian," Harold said lamely.

"So I see." And then her eyes caught Thelma's. "Oh, hello."

"Marian, this is Thelma."

"Hi, Thelma," she twinkled.

"Oh, Mrs. Fouts," cried Thelma. "Harold is having trouble with his car."

"Harold, did you pump the gas pedal?"

"No, I'll try it."

He did and the car sputtered Marian smiled pleasantly at Thelma.

"Try it again, Harold."

He did and the car's motor cried out against the Fates.

The enormity of the situation was just hitting Thelma, and the humor of it, Marian.

The two women looked at each other. Thelma was at a slight disadvantage. She was sitting in the front seat with a big bag on her lap. Marian looked down at her and smiled, "Thelma, be happy."

All that Thelma could say, with a weak smile, was, "You seem to know how to get things started."

"My life story," laughed Marian. And she waved them goodbye.

When she returned, Leona had everyone and all of the picnic stuff stowed in the car.

"You certainly handled that one," she commented.

"Leona, you know something funny? They were made for each other," she responded with a little smile.

CHAPTER SEVENTY FIVE

Tony saw the Whaler as it rounded into the marina. He ran toward the dock.

"You're early," he cried. "Where's the yacht?"

"There's been an accident," Rizzo said tersely. "Here, help this guy put the cases into your truck. In the back."

He snapped at the Whaler pilot, "Help him. Then Tony, just put your truck in the storage area near the boathouse and stay with it. Millie, you and the General come with me."

They walked quickly toward the boathouse to a stairway which led to the apartment.

The "parrot" was reluctant to leave the goods. Looking over his shoulder, he sputtered again about wanting a car to take the bags back to town.

"Forget it," said Rizzo.

The accident had played right into Rizzo's hands. It was all very neat. It suggested that Rizzo might have been meeting with the insurrectionists quartered in San Francisco. Whether this was the truth or not, except for the presence of the General, everything had worked out for Rizzo.

"Millie, fix me something to eat. Here, General, fix yourself a drink." And he opened the bar.

Rizzo turned and ran down the stairs bellowing for Tony whom he found descending from the cab of his behemoth. Breathlessly, he ordered Tony to bring up two suitcases and lock his vehicle.

In this breathing space, the General took off his gaudy uniform tunic and sat down in his silk Philippine shirt. He looked up as Rizzo returned.

"Mr. Rizzo, it has all gone wrong."

"Not at all, General."

"How are we to be paid?"

"Relax. You'll be paid, and very quickly."

"I don't understand. We were supposed to handle this on the yacht."

"You're quite right. And now the yacht is in virtual quarantine."

"What happened to it? What happened to the President?" His boss was second in his concern.

"When I heard the explosion, I had only one thought and that was to get those suitcases off and into our fast boat. Luckily, Millie was handy and I was able to get her off, too."

Millie heard this from the kitchen and she yelled in, "Thanks a lot, baby. What now?"

She came to the door.

"We'll sell as much of this stuff as we can today. The money we can use. The powder is a headache." He smiled at his almost clever play on words.

The General had a single-track mind.

"When do we get paid?"

"General, I just explained that you will be paid. Doesn't that suggest anything to you?"

"Look, Mr. Rizzo," the General was catching on. "If I don't pay them, I don't live long enough to count the money."

"We'll try to help you, General."

While Rizzo, Millie, and the General were making themselves uncomfortable at home, Tony was able to talk to the narc agents and inform them of the new developments and of the fact that Rizzo had brought along six suitcases of snow, which were in the compactor.

They had already picked up a garbled message about the ship blowing up.

The narcs told Tony to play along. They wanted to wait and pick up as many buyers as they could.

Tony started loping back down the hill to return to the boathouse.

CHAPTER SEVENTY SIX

The driver of the limousine carrying Spisak and Dale Harris knew how to get to Highway 101 over the Richmond-San Rafael Bridge. He lost no time. Cutting off the freeway at the San Anselmo exit, he found the overpass leading to the abandoned marina.

As they slowed down to make the approach, Spisak noticed Tony sprinting down the road to some buildings, one of which answered the description of the boathouse.

The shiny limousine pulled up alongside him.

"Hey, Tony!" Spisak called to him. "Where's the action?"

The car stopped and Tony jumped into the front seat. He told the driver to make the loop and head back for the highway. Spisak did not dispute the order.

The chauffeur, directed by Tony, drove the car around the bend where several other vehicles were stopped off the road.

"Your narcs are operating from here," Tony stated. "One of them will fill you in. I've got to get back." He ran down the hill.

The plan of attack was outlined to Chief Narcotics Agent, Dale Harris. Harris agreed and took over command.

Tony returned to the boathouse. He heard Rizzo yelling again for the bags. He picked out two of the suitcases and ran upstairs with them.

CHAPTER SEVENTY SEVEN

Rizzo placed the bags on a table which had been cleared. The General came forward and as Rizzo opened the top suitcase, he inspected it. They removed some newspaper which covered the material. There it all was, put together in neat little cellophane bags. The General nodded and Rizzo smiled. They then tongue-tested the contents, repeating the performance two or three more times until both were satisfied.

"Good stuff!"

"I hope, the best." The General gave a little bow. "Now, how about payment, and then I can leave."

Not knowing what the outcome would be relative to the confrontation and the payoff, Rizzo had tried to delay the moment. He reached into his pocket and pulled out half of his supply of Treasury bills. These he reluctantly gave to the General.

"But, there is more," said the General with his hand still extended.

"Of course there is," agreed a fast-thinking Rizzo, "but we must wait for the buyers."

Just then, the buzzer made its peculiar noise. Rizzo slipped the suitcase closed and locked it. Then he dragged both of the bags into the next room. He then went downstairs. Two men were waiting. They were recognized by Rizzo as his "Vegas" customers.

"Come on up," he invited. The men followed him.

"O.K., what have you got?" the older man asked.

"The best," smiled Rizzo.

"I'll be the judge of that."

The visitors took seats around the table. Rizzo went into the other room, returning with one of the open packages.

"Try this," and he proffered the envelope.

"Vegas" tasted. "How much 'ya got like this?" he queried.

"What's your budget?"

"Plenty."

"O.K. How about 40 kilos at 2 mil 4?"

"Not so much. 30 at 1 mil 5."

"Can't. I'm not in this alone. Twenty-five at 1 mil 7."

"All right."

And so the first deal was made.

The second man was carrying a large briefcase. He made payment. Rizzo counted out the packages. "Vegas" departed, thinking they were departing for Nevada.

As their car proceeded up the one-way road

to the freeway on-ramp, they were detained by the narcs. This arrest was handled at a place completely screened from the parking area and the entrance.

Not long after "Vegas" had departed, three more customers arrived. Rizzo recognized one as Sacramento and the other two from Santa Rosa.

Similar deals were struck for more money.

They departed and were detained.

And so the next two hours went by. The supply lessened and the money pile grew.

The General, who had never observed deals at this level, sat quietly in the corner. Finally, seven and a half million dollars had been collected. Rizzo called Tony.

"Call a cab for the General, will you?"

He turned to the General. "The deal was twelve million. Here's cash and Treasury notes. I want you to sign that you have received this money."

He gave a piece of paper and a pen to the General, who was shaking. Then he brought forward a heavy grocery box into which he piled the money.

"There you go. Tony, take the General downstairs and wait with him until the cab comes."

The General put on his tunic and Rizzo gave him a raincoat so he would not look so obvious.

"Your party is scheduled for the Stanford Court. Good luck."

During this, the General was breathless. After

counting the money by packets, he had signed the paper with a flourish and crawled into the raincoat.

"That's done, Mr. Rizzo. My people will be happy that they did business with you."

"I hope so."

The parrot-faced General clutched the box for dear life. As Tony and the General opened the door to go downstairs, the door bell rang twice. As they descended, three more men came up the stairs. Tony recognized that they were expected.

Rizzo had just told Millie that the rest of the money would be for them. In walked three southern California types.

"Hi, Rizzo. What have you got?"

"You must have thought something was cooking, or you wouldn't have come up."

"We were told good, top stuff."

"You can say that again."

"The boss wants a heavy load."

"You've come to the right place."

"What'cha got?"

"What'cha bring?"

"Enough."

"Well, how would you like a suitcase at 5 mil?"

"Probably could use."

"You got it."

A large briefcase was put on the table.

"Let's see the stuff."

Rizzo went into the other room and brought

back a package. It was sampled all around. The deal was made, which left Rizzo with seven kilos from the first case. The rest of his loot rested in the garbage truck. He brought out the suitcase. The men went through it, sampling here and there. Finally, they snapped it shut and pushed the briefcase to Rizzo.

It was Rizzo's turn. He riffled through the money, occasionally holding a bill up to the light. Much of it was in bearer bonds.

"This seems all right. Tell'em hello for me in L.A."

George Rizzo didn't even see the fellows to the door. He was busy planning his next move.

CHAPTER SEVENTY EIGHT

One of the narc agents came up to Tony downstairs and advised him that the Chief wanted to take the other four suitcases into custody now.

"O.K.," agreed Tony. "I'll just bring the whole rig up there."

He went back into the warehouse and revved his vehicle into action. Upstairs, Rizzo called to Millie, "Come on, we're leaving!"

"In what?"

"I have one of my cars in the garage here."

"Let me tidy up."

"The hell with that, c'mon. Bring this bag," and he pointed to the satchel carrying what was left over from the snow. "I'll go down and take care of Tony."

He picked up his bulky, money-laden briefcase.

He went down the staircase two at a time. At the bottom, he saw Tony driving the rig out of the warehouse area. He went after him.

"Hey, Tony!" Rizzo yelled. "Where the hell are you going?

"I'm taking myself back to town."

"You're what?"

"I'm going to take this stuff back to town."

"The hell you are!" cried Rizzo and, still clutching his briefcase, he jumped onto the running board of the slow-moving truck.

He smashed Tony in the face with his free hand and tried to grab the key, but missed. Tony gave him a push and Rizzo fell to the ground. He tried to scramble up, still holding onto the briefcase. He began fumbling with his other hand in his pocket, trying to extricate his gun.

Tony braked the rig and leapt from the cab. Rizzo tried to hit him with the briefcase. Blows were exchanged. Rizzo ran to the rear of the truck still fumbling in his pocket. This was a ridiculous confrontation when you consider the size of Tony and the smallness of Rizzo. But, Rizzo was fast and he was very strong.

Tony began yelling for the narcs but continued after Rizzo. Rizzo finally managed to pull out his gun and Tony closed with him, grabbing his arm. He hit him heavily in the face and Rizzo fell back against the tailgate of the truck.

The force with which he had been hit knocked Rizzo off balance. The gun fell from his hand. Tony swung a haymaker. This time, Rizzo and his briefcase went right up in the air, his free hand clawing to save his fall.

By mistake, he hit the safety button on the

rig and the machine roared. On coming down, Rizzo fell across the rail into the iron monster's mouth.

Millie had just come down, carrying her coat and the small bag. What she saw horrified her. Rizzo, struggling to hold onto the rail lost his fight and was completely engulfed in the machine, along with the briefcase which he clutched to his body just as he disappeared.

Tony, who had stumbled after delivering his blow to Rizzo's face, looked up from the ground in disbelief.

Two narcotics agents ran into the scene. Tony yelled for them to turn off the truck's motor. One of the men leapt into the cab but could not immediately locate the key. For a short period, there was a terrible sound of the machine making heavy scraping noises, accompanied by the screams of Rizzo as he tried to free himself from his revolving prison.

With a final crunch, only the scraping noise could be heard above the rumble of the motor. At last, Tony was able to pull the keys from the dashboard. The great truck shuddered and was silent.

Millie fainted.

CHAPTER SEVENTY NINE

After a fast limousine ride from Alameda, the President and his wife arrived at the Stanford Court. With no baggage. The room clerk would make an exception. The local stores would be able to declare a holiday once these two finished their wardrobe shopping. Merchant princes would become merchant kings.

The Commodore of the St. Francis Yacht Club returned to the Basin with the San Francisco Chief of Protocol and his dog. He immediately assumed command of the situation from the Club's flight deck. By the time they arrived at the Club House, the President's beautiful cruise ship was no more and the Mayor's yacht was long out of sight. The Commodore wondered whether or not the hulk would be a menace to navigation. He'd get a committee going on that one. The Chief of Protocol was disappointed that his lunch-hosting job was cancelled, but was relieved that he had left the reception job on the yacht to others.

"Ah, well," he said to his dog, "there'll be other luncheons and other Presidents, but next time I'll see to it that they arrive by railroad train!"

CHAPTER EIGHTY

As darkness closed in at the marina, Tony ran from the truck to alert the agents as to what had happened. Millie was unconsciously reliving the horror she had just witnessed.

The agents had rounded up every person who had visited and then left the boathouse. The loudest yells were coming from the General, who was trying to invoke diplomatic immunity. The next loudest were coming from the unhappy taxicab driver who felt unjustly put upon. All of these prisoners had been handcuffed in and to various narc vehicles. They were a surly group.

"We'll take 'em back to town," Chief Narcotics Agent Harris informed Tony above the noise.

"Before you go, please come down and see what has happened here. Rizzo was trying to escape. I knocked him into the garbage scupper here and he accidently released the safety. He's probably in a million pieces, along with the four suitcases of snow!"

All of this was described as they jogged downhill to the garbage truck. People from the restaurant now began to try to help Millie.

"Some guy grabbed at her purse and then ran up the hill," a beery-type was babbling.

"What the hell is this garbage truck doing here?" was asked above the confusion.

"Where are they when you need them?"

Someone had gone to call the police. The action to this moment had worked so smoothly that no one had thought to alert the local cops or the Highway Patrol. Dale Harris went over to Millie and satisfied himself that she was all right.

"How do you feel, honey?" he tried to say in a low, soothing voice.

"Oh, God!" she sobbed. "George, little Georgie. Just gone, right in front of me. One minute fighting for his life, then, gone."

"You'll be all right, lady. Calm down."

"Listen, buster, I'm fine. But how about him? Can you get him out? I think someone ought to look."

Dale Harris took up her suggestion. He asked Tony if it would be possible to look into the maw of this behemoth.

"Better wait until we're back in the garage," advised Tony.

"Any chance the guy's alive?"

"None at all. He's a mixture of snow, and blood now, and you'd better just wait until later."

Actually, George was pulverized blood, snow, and money.

Just then, the scream of sirens could be heard and the police and the Highway Patrol arrived in swirls of dust and pebbles. One man nearly drove his vehicle right off the dock.

"O.K., O.K., what happened here?" one police officer barked as he saw Millie's banged-up appearance. "You been attacked, lady?"

A Highway Patrol Sergeant took her by the arm.

The local policeman bristled a little at the Highway Patrolman. Tony went up to the California Highway Patrol Sergeant.

"Sergeant, this is a long story . . ." he began.

Dale Harris came over. "Sergeant, we're having a drug bust here. It's big."

"When will you guys start tying us in? We could help you, you know."

"I know, I know. We expected one thing to happen here and before we could do anything about it, the whole ball game changed."

"You could have called us," the Sergeant insisted.

"What we thought was going to happen didn't. All these guys started trooping in."

"We like to be alerted, you know." The Sergeant wanted to get his point across.

"Picking up these guys was like shooting fish in a barrel. One after the other we stopped them up there and arrested them."

"Arrested them? On what authority?"

Dale Harris pulled out his badge and I.D.

"O.K.," said the miffed Sergeant. "Next time, let us in on it, see?"

As he said that, one more car skidded into the now-crowded parking lot. It was the Sheriff.

He jumped out of his steaming car and immediately questioned the presence of the garbage rig.

"They're supposed to be here on Tuesdays and Fridays. What's the matter? Did it break down?"

Up to this point, nothing had been said to the police about its grizzly contents. Tony stepped forward.

"We've had an accident here."

The Sergeant standing nearby who, up to this time, had no report pad in front of him, quickly pulled one from his pocket. The word "accident" had triggered his conditioned reflex.

It was nearly nightfall and so the rest of the inquisition went on benefited by police car headlights. The Sergeant turned to Tony, pencil and pad in hand.

"O.K., spill it, fella."

As Tony started, Dale Harris came into the light.

"Sergeant, a full report will be made to you. But, as for now, I must exert my jurisdiction. This man may be charged with a Federal crime and he also may become a government witness. I'm not going to permit him to say anymore."

The Highway Patrol Sergeant opened his mouth, closed it, and looked over at the Sheriff, who just shrugged.

Taking the Sheriff and the Highway Patrol

Sergeant to one side, Harris said, "Look, you can help us. We need some police vans for the guys who have been taken prisoner up the hill."

The Highway Patrol Sergeant called over one of the officers and gave him the needed orders.

Harris continued, "Over there is a boathouse which we have not been able to search. If we could have some of your boys help us with that, it would be appreciated."

He didn't expect to find anything, but this gave everyone something to do. The vans arrived, and the prisoners, including the General, were loaded in and locked up. It was decided to let the taxicab driver go after taking his name and badge number. The others were transported to the Federal Building's security center.

Millie had been on the outside of all of this discussion and was nearly lost in the shadows. Tony found her and offered her a ride back to town with him in the rig. She accepted, notwithstanding the truck's unusual load. Up to this point, the narcs thought Millie was Tony's friend.

The narcotics officer directed Tony to the Federal Building garage, where the truck would be impounded. Tony crawled into the cab. Its engine roared.

Agents met them when they arrived at the garage and a second guard was put on the truck until such time as its contents could be strained. Literally.

As Millie left the cab of the truck, she went around to the rear of it and put her hand on the rail. The narcotics man standing nearest to her heard her whisper, "Well, so long, Georgie . . . it could have been great. But, that's the way the cookie crum . . . crumb . . ." She could not finish. She was taken into custody.

EPILOGUE

The President and his wife went on to Washington, D.C. looking very American. They eventually bought a piece of property near Wheeling, West Virginia and took up residence there.

The dope dealers and Donno Ferreri all went to the penitentiary, where it was reported that most of them made very bad prisoners, which added to their discomfort. Ferreri tried to involve the President's wife, but nobody took him seriously.

Dale Harris became the smallest Administrator in the history of the Drug Enforcement Administration.

George Rizzo's experience in the meatgrinder was put down as "accidental death while perpetrating a felony."

The mixture of snow, blood, and money was finally cleaned up, placed in new containers, and sold to a large chemical supply house which put the material in form for legal use—sixty two years of it!

The old Irishman who owned the great garbage truck, not one to overlook a bet, put it on exhibit where the curious—paying a dollar and fifty cents—could take a look at it, children fifty cents. The more thrifty but curious members of the general public looked a second time at passing garbage vehicles without charge.

The yacht Captain went to jail for harboring criminals.

The Mayor's secretary recovered, but walks with a slight limp.

Mayor Belpierre was unmasked by the widows and older orphans of San Francisco. After a time as the government's guest at Lompoc, he retired to a little home he had in Stinson Beach, purchased for him from a widower's fund which he had established long ago.

Mr. Murphy left San Francisco hastily when the story broke. Candy stayed. The associates of Mr. Murphy in Miami, upon his arrival, gave him a pair of large cement shoes, and he was never heard of again.

The brave Filipinos who had operated the fast black boat which eviscerated the President's ship were never identified

Juan Loredo eventually returned home to a hero's welcome. When he came to power, he even tried, tongue-in-cheek, to get reparations for the loss of the former President's cruise ship. The matter is still before a court of maritime claims.

Marian and Harold took advantage of California's lenient dissolution laws.

Harold married Thelma, who retired from her job on a good pension. Harold qualified in the Civil Service exams as a city gardener. He presently has daytime employment in Golden Gate Park's conservatory. His eyes do not bother him any more in the light of the conservatory.

Marian found everything she ever wanted or needed in her husband, Lowell Spisak.

Spisak did not remain long with the Federal government. He decided to practice law and eventually became the Lieutenant Governor of the State of California. It was said that his wife had a way with senior politicians.

Tony and Leona married immediately. They subsequently had three children. He, taking his mother's recipes, set up a fine, though small, Italian restaurant and began handling garbage in its unrefined form.

Millie, exonerated, had her living room window and the image of Coit Tower. After George Rizzo, that was enough for her.

In San Francisco, the side streets remain the same. Row on row. However, those privy to this tale can now appreciate that a mouse may not only look at a king, but may glut at the same smorgasbord of sexual license. The bluebird of happiness is everywhere.

In our own democratic land, it is heartening

to know that excitement, love, intrigue, and lust are equally shared between the rich and the others, without regard to the view from the bedroom window.